That's a GREAT Answer!

Teaching Literature Response to K-3, ELL, and Struggling Readers

Nancy N. Boyles

Maupin House

That's a GREAT Answer!
Teaching Literature Response to K-3, ELL, and Struggling Readers
©2007 by Nancy N. Boyles

Library of Congress Cataloging-in-Publication Data

Boyles, Nancy N., 1948-
  That's a great answer! : teaching literature response to K-3, ELL, and
struggling readers / Nancy N. Boyles.
      p. cm.
  Includes bibliographical references.
  ISBN 978-1-934338-12-4 (pbk.)
  1. Reading comprehension--Study and teaching--United States. 2. Motivation
in education--United States. I. Title.
LB1050.45.B69 2007
372.47--dc22
                          2007036052

Also by Nancy N. Boyles:
Constructing Meaning through Kid-friendly Comprehension Strategy Instruction
Teaching Written Response to Text
Hands-On Literacy Coaching

Contact Nancy N. Boyles through Maupin House Publishing for workshops or conference appearances.

Maupin House publishes professional resources for K-12 educators. Contact us for tailored, in-school training or to schedule an author for a workshop or conference. Visit www.maupinhouse.com for free lesson plan downloads.

Maupin House Publishing, Inc.
2416 NW 71 Place
Gainesville, FL 32653

www.maupinhouse.com
800-524-0634
352-373-5588
352-373-5546 (fax)
info@maupinhouse.com

10 9 8 7 6 5 4 3 2 1

Dedication

This book is dedicated to all of the teachers and administrators
in districts throughout Connecticut
whose paths have crossed mine in one way or another over many years—
district workshops, classroom visits, CT Reading Conference presentations,
and the occasional "summit meeting" around my kitchen table
(complete with a glass of wine!).
Thank you for your dedication to teaching comprehension strategies and response to text
in authentic and meaningful ways.
You make me proud to be a Connecticut educator.

Table Of Contents

PART II: TIPS, TEXTS, AND TEMPLATES FOR APPROACHING READING-COMPREHENSION OBJECTIVES

Chapter 9: Examining the Content and Structure of Text   140

ON THE CD

Introduction

What's the problem?

How can we get past the one-word answer or blank stare we get from many primary-grade students, struggling readers, and English language learners when we ask them a question about a story or nonfiction text we have read to them or one they have read themselves? It's frustrating! It's also worrisome since most students beginning in the third grade must now take state-mandated literacy tests that often require written response to text in short or even long answers. We feel a sense of urgency in helping our youngest students respond to literature thoughtfully. We feel this same urgency for struggling readers at higher grade levels and for English language learners who may understand a piece of literature but lack reading and writing competencies to express their understanding in writing.

What is the goal of this book, and who will it help?

It is certainly true that writing good answers helps to boost literacy scores on state assessments. But teaching students to answer questions well goes way beyond just teaching to the test. Responding to open-ended questions is a regular part of a student's academic life from the very earliest grades right through college graduation—from *Little Red Riding Hood* to *The Red Badge of Courage*. Learning to respond meaningfully to text is a skill that students will use every day, not just on test day.

This book is for primary-grade teachers who want to introduce their students to response to text in a way that empowers them right from the start. It also supports struggling readers and writers and English language learners in the intermediate and upper grades who fall short of meeting grade-level literacy standards. In this book, I present simple, research-based strategies to move these students toward independently producing quality written responses to open-ended comprehension questions.

How does this book support literature response?

As teachers we long to praise students for their good responses to literature. "That's a great answer!" we announce to a third grader whose summary of a text includes all of the story's important components in a short, succinct manner. So how do we help primary and struggling students write great answers to open-ended comprehension questions?
The foundation of a great answer—whether oral or written—is built upon great objectives, great books, great instruction, and great discussions. The first four chapters of Part I address each of these instructional components, while the final chapter, Chapter 5, shows you how to assess both written and oral responses.

The four chapters in Part II provide very concrete guidance for supporting students in acquiring the strategies they need to craft high-quality answers to open-ended questions—all by themselves. To simplify this process, the twelve broad objectives from Chapter 1 are broken down into forty specific and measurable open-ended questions. The broad objectives are also grouped into one of the four thinking strands aligned with the current standards of the National Assessment of Educational Progress (NAEP) and can be correlated with the literacy objectives of *any* state curriculum. Chapters 6, 7, 8, and 9 each cover one of these strands.

Each open-ended question includes teaching tips, a bibliography of picture books aligned with the question, and a template that specifies the reading strategy (how to locate the best evidence in the text), the writing strategy (the criteria for producing a quality response), and an answer frame to scaffold students as they initially practice the response. The answer frames are suitable for students just getting started with open-ended responses.

I have also included a bibliography at the end of this book that lists all books alphabetically, along with possible objectives matched to each text.

The CD that accompanies this book includes all of the answer frames for the 40 open-ended questions in Chapters 6 through 9, as well as the rubrics, criteria charts, and planners from Chapters 3 through 5, useful to both teachers and students for their classroom literacy work. See the Table of Contents for a complete listing of the CD files.

Moving on

I know you are tempted to skip Part I, the first five chapters of this book, and go directly to Part II. In fact, what you would *really* like to do is go directly to the answer frame you need tomorrow and scurry to the duplicating machine to run enough copies for everyone in your class. Please resist the urge to do this.

Without this background, the frames will become just another bunch of activity sheets (we used to call them "dittos") that will keep kids busy but won't serve any real purpose in improving student learning.

With that thought, let's begin this journey where all good teaching begins: with great learning objectives.

PART I:
GETTING TO GREAT ANSWERS

Literacy objectives for open-ended response: What, why, how

The National Assessment of Educational Progress (NAEP) assesses a sample of thousands of students in reading in grades four, eight, and twelve from *all* states in alternate years. Some states, in an effort to align their standards with NAEP, have adopted this framework to organize their reading-comprehension objectives. By doing so, they hope that there will be a closer correlation between the results of their state literacy assessment, and the findings of NAEP for their state. They can then address deficit areas and hopefully do better in the next round of NAEP assessments.

Because all states are ultimately accountable to the NAEP (also known as our "Nation's Report Card"), I chose their framework by which to organize the broad objectives. The framework used by the NAEP includes four thinking strands:

- ■ A: Forming a general understanding
- ■ B: Developing an interpretation
- ■ C: Making reader/text connections
- ■ D: Examining content and structure

Bear in mind that the NAEP does not assign the actual objectives within each strand. For the specific objectives, I used Connecticut's classification system. Your state might place certain objectives within different strands. It really doesn't matter. What does matter is that we teach these objectives and that we teach them well.

It would be impossible for this book (or any book) to feature all of the objectives suitable for open-ended literature response. There are simply too many of them. The objectives selected here "made the cut" for three reasons.

- ■ They are broad, generic, and can be applied to a wide range of both fiction and nonfiction literature.
- ■ They are appropriate for the students that this book targets: primary-grade students, struggling readers and writers beyond the primary level, and English language learners.
- ■ They address different ways of thinking and processing text.

Making sense of the strands, objectives, and questions

Here's how to make sense of everything in this book and the way it is organized. First, note the strands. As described previously, there are four of them. It is important to understand that they do not represent *levels* of thinking. In other words, they do not build in ascending order. Here, "B" strand objectives are not necessarily more difficult than "A" strand objectives. They are simply *different ways* of thinking.

Next, note the objectives within each strand. For example, the first "A" objective is *A1: Main idea and theme*. The second "A" objective is *A2: Characters, problem/solution, setting*. Each strand has two to four related objectives.

Each objective is then divided into measurable, open-ended questions: *A1-a: What lesson does _____ learn in this story? (fiction); A1-b: What is the theme of this story? (fiction)*. In order to be useful, objectives MUST be measurable!

Take the first objective, *A1: Main idea and theme*. How do you measure students' expertise with that? You can't! It's too broad. There are too many different ways of approaching it. By contrast, if you wish to measure students' competence in coming up with another good title for a story or article *(A1-d)*, is that measurable? Yes, it is. There are specific things for students to think about as they read and a clear progression of steps involved in writing a good response to this question.

Thinking of the questions as the specific, measurable parts of the objective will be helpful to both teachers and students. Students will be less intimidated because now they know *exactly* what counts as success. Likewise, teachers will find that they can assess students' work more efficiently because they know precisely what to look for in their students' responses.

An almost-final note: If you post your objective in your classroom for students to see, as teachers are required to do in some schools, post the specific, open-ended questions rather than the broader objective.

The most important note of all: In the interest of not going to jail, I want to say clearly that I did not identify either the broad objectives within each strand *(A1, A2, A3,* etc.) or the open-ended questions *(A1-a, A1-b, A1-c,* etc.). These were the inventions of the Connecticut State Department of Education. The full document from which this framework was adapted, the *Language Arts Handbook for Generation Four of the Connecticut Mastery Test*, may be accessed through the Connecticut State DOE's website.

While I did not create the strands, broad objectives, and open-ended questions listed on the following pages, I do take responsibility for everything in this book that follows this list. As I work with teachers in their districts and in my graduate classes, they talk to me about the things that are hard for them in the teaching of literacy. Addressing state reading-comprehension objectives is a source of anxiety that I hear about a lot. The resources I have developed in this book are an attempt to reduce that stress.

Here is the list of objectives and open-ended questions for each of the four strands. Next to each question in parentheses is an indication of whether the question is appropriate for fiction, nonfiction, or both fiction and nonfiction texts.

The "A" strand: Forming a general understanding	
A1: Main idea and theme	**A1-a**: What lesson does _____ learn in this story? (fiction) **A1-b**: What is the theme of this story? (fiction) **A1-c**: What is this book/article mainly about? (nonfiction) **A1-d**: What would be another good title for this story/text? (fiction, nonfiction)
A2: Characters, problem/solution, setting	**A2-a**: Using information in the story, write a brief description of how _____ felt when _____. (fiction) **A2-b**: What is _____'s main problem in the story? Give details from the story to support your answer. (fiction) **A2-c**: How did _____ solve his/her problem? Give details from the story to support your answer. (fiction) **A2-d**: How did _____ change from the beginning to the end of the story? (fiction) **A2-e**: What is the setting of this story? Give details from the story to support your answer. (fiction)
A3: Summarizing	**A3-a**: Briefly summarize this story. (fiction) **A3-b**: Summarize the main things that happened in this [book]. (fiction, nonfiction) **A3-c**: Briefly summarize this article/informational text. (nonfiction)
A4: Predicting	**A4-a**: Predict what will happen next in this story. (fiction) **A4-b**: If the author added another paragraph to the end of the story (or article), it would <u>most likely</u> tell about _____. Use information from the story (or article) to support your answer. (fiction, nonfiction)

The "B" strand: Developing an interpretation	
B1: Identify or infer the author's use of structure/ organizational patterns	**B1-a**: What caused _____ to happen in the story? (fiction) **B1-b**: What happened at the beginning, in the middle, and at the end of the story or informational text? (fiction, nonfiction) **B1-c**: Compare these two characters: _____ and _____. (fiction) **B1-d**: Can this part of the [story/text] be described as: a definition, a description, an explanation, a conversation, an opinion, an argument, or a comparison? How do you know? (fiction, nonfiction)
B2: Draw conclusions about the author's purpose for choosing a genre or for including or omitting specific details in text	**B2-a**: Why does the author include paragraph ___? (fiction, nonfiction) **B2-b**: Why did the author write a [poem/story/informational article/nonfiction book] about this? (fiction, nonfiction)
B3: Use evidence from the text to support a conclusion	**B3-a**: Prove that [character/person] is very _____. (fiction, nonfiction) **B3-b**: Which facts show that _____? (nonfiction)

The "C" strand: Making reader/text connections	
C1: Connect the text to personal experience, another text, or the outside world	**C1-a**: Think about someone who was [helpful]. Tell how that experience was like the experience of _____ in the story. (fiction) **C1-b**: Make a personal connection. Show how something that happened in the story is like something that happened in your own life. (fiction) **C1-c**: Which character in the story would you like to know and why? (fiction) **C1-d**: Using information in the story, explain whether you would ever want to _____. (fiction)
C2: Make a personal response to the text	**C2-a**: Which part of the [story/article] do you think was *most* important? Use information from the [story/article] to explain why you chose that part. (fiction, nonfiction) **C2-b**: Which part of this [story/article] was most interesting or surprising to you? Why? (fiction, nonfiction) **C2-c**: Did you like this [story/article]? Why or why not? (fiction, nonfiction) **C2-d**: What was your first reaction to this text? Explain. (fiction, nonfiction)

The "D" strand: Examining content and structure	
D1: Examine the author's craft	**D1-a**: Choose [2] words from paragraph ___ that help you picture the _____. (fiction, nonfiction) **D1-b**: Choose a simile and explain why the author chose that simile. (fiction, nonfiction) **D1-c**: How did the author create humor in paragraph ___? (fiction) **D1-d**: Give an example of personification in paragraph ___. (fiction) **D1-e**: Do you think the author made this story believable? Why or why not? (fiction)
D2: Extend the text	**D2-a**: What two questions would you like to ask the author that were not answered in this text? (fiction, nonfiction) **D2-b**: Imagine you are going to give a talk to your class about _____. What two points would you be sure to include in your speech? (nonfiction) **D2-c**: Using information in the text, write a paragraph that could have appeared in ____'s journal after _____ occurred. (fiction, nonfiction)
D3: Show that you understand what was important to an author or character	**D3-a**: How does the author/character show that _____ is important to him/her? (fiction, nonfiction) **D3-b**: How are your customs different from the customs described in this story? (fiction)

Deciding which objectives and questions to teach

Now that you have a wide selection of possible objectives, where will you start? Choosing comprehension objectives should always depend on what students need right now in order to improve their understanding of text. That does not mean, however, that selecting appropriate comprehension objectives is simply a matter of figuring out what to teach tomorrow. Good teachers also develop a plan for how they will embed *all* of the objectives they need to cover within their year-long literacy curriculum.

The charts at the end of this chapter list possible objectives to be introduced in each grade, K-3. Note that these are only *suggestions*. You will need to decide as an individual teacher, as a grade-level team, or as a school or district whether these suggestions are too ambitious, not ambitious enough, or just right for the students *you* teach.

The objectives are listed in terms of grade level, but they can also be considered in terms of their level of difficulty for struggling readers and English language learners. Objectives indicated for kindergarten would be most appropriate for the neediest older students, while those objectives recommended for third grade would be suitable for more capable readers working below grade level.

A couple of observations may be apparent as you study these four grade-level charts. First, at every grade level, students work with "A," "B," "C," and "D" objectives. It is important to expose students at every grade level to thinking processes in all four thinking strands. It would be a mistake to try to march through the strands one at a time, for instance, expecting students to master all of the objectives in the "A" strand before moving on to the "B" strand. Students at *all* grade levels can, and should, have the opportunity to think both concretely and abstractly.

With that in mind, one might also observe that most of the "A" strand objectives are introduced in the earlier grades, while many "D" strand objectives come later. While it is true that these are thinking *strands* and not thinking *levels*, it is pretty obvious that identifying things like characters, settings, and problems (A2) are easier for students and more concrete than determining the values that underlie an author's or character's motives (D3) which requires very abstract thinking.

Local educators should choose how teachers distribute these objectives over the year. In Connecticut, where I teach, we are given information from our state department of education about which objectives will be assessed most heavily at different grade levels. Districts that "teach smart" look at this information and determine which objectives will receive the most emphasis in a particular grade. They establish their pacing guide accordingly with one or two specific objectives "featured" each month at most grade levels. The featured objectives are taught explicitly and assessed at the end of the month (or marking period) to determine whether students have mastered them. All objectives taught previously are continually reviewed through literature discussions and written responses to keep them fresh in students' minds.

Rather than featuring a single objective in kindergarten and first grade, it is wise to repeatedly teach a few objectives throughout the year to provide continued exposure to different ways of thinking about and responding to text. Students are not expected to "master" an objective in the traditional sense as in these early grades their developmental level changes so rapidly. After all, a personal connection to text in September looks different indeed from the kind of connection that same kindergarten student may make in March.

Once an objective is introduced, it should be reinforced at each subsequent grade level so that the curriculum spirals with increasing levels of rigor as students move from grade to grade. For example, teachers will need to decide what counts as meeting grade-level standards for summarizing text in the third grade and how that differs from the criteria used to assess a summary in grade two.

Moving on

Most comprehension objectives can be manageable for students in the early primary grades as well as older struggling readers. But for that we will need the right texts, quality instruction, oral discussion that precedes written response, and clear criteria for good answers. We will look next at choosing great books to teach our comprehension objectives.

OBJECTIVES INTRODUCED AT EACH GRADE LEVEL

	Kindergarten
A: Forming a general understanding	**Introduce:** **A1-a**: What lesson does _____ learn in this story? (fiction) **A2-a**: Using information in the story, give a brief description of how _____ felt when _____. (fiction) **A2-b**: What is _____'s main problem in the story? Give details from the story to support your answer. (fiction) **A2-c**: How did _____ solve his/her problem? Give details from the story to support your answer. (fiction) **A2-e**: What is the setting of this story? Give details from the story to support your answer. (fiction) **A4-a**: Predict what will happen next in the story. (fiction)
B: Developing an interpretation	**Introduce:** **B1-b**: What happened at the beginning, in the middle, and at the end of the story or informational text? (fiction, nonfiction) **B1-c**: Compare these characters: _____ and _____. (fiction) **B3-a**: Prove that [character] is very _____. (fiction)
C: Making reader/text connections	**Introduce:** **C1-a**: Think about someone who was [helpful]. Tell how that experience was like the experience of _____ in the story. (fiction) **C2-c**: Did you like this [story/article]? Why or why not? (fiction, nonfiction)
D: Examining content and structure	**Introduce:** **D2-a**: What two questions would you like to ask the author that were not answered in this text? (fiction, nonfiction)

First Grade	
A: Forming a general understanding	**Continue all previous objectives; introduce:** **A1-c**: What is this book/article mainly about? (nonfiction) **A1-d**: What would be another good title for this story/text? (fiction, nonfiction) **A2-d**: How did _____ change from the beginning to the end of the story? (fiction) **A4-b**: If the author added another paragraph to the end of the story (or article), it would <u>most likely</u> tell about _____. Use information fro the story (or article) to support your answer. (fiction, nonfiction)
B: Developing an interpretation	**Continue all previous objectives; introduce:** **B1-a**: What caused _____ to happen in the story? (fiction) **B3-b**: Which facts show that _____? (nonfiction)
C: Making reader/ text connections	**Continue all previous objectives; introduce:** **C1-c**: Which character in the story would you like to know and why? (fiction) **C1-d**: Using information in the story, explain whether you would ever want to _____. (fiction) **C2-b**: Which part of this [story/article] was most interesting or surprising to you? Why? (fiction, nonfiction) **C2-d**: What was your first reaction to this text? Explain. (fiction, nonfiction)
D: Examining content and structure	**Continue all previous objectives; introduce:** **D1-a**: Choose [2] words from paragraph ___ that help you picture the ___. (fiction, nonfiction) **D1-e**: Do you think the author made this story believable? Why or why not? (fiction)

Second Grade	
A: Forming a general understanding	**Continue all previous objectives; introduce:** **A1-b**: What is the theme of this story (fiction)? **A3-a**: Briefly summarize this story. (fiction) **A3-b**: Summarize the main things that happened in this [book]. (fiction, nonfiction) **A3-c**: Briefly summarize this article/informational text. (nonfiction)
B: Developing an interpretation	**Continue all previous objectives; introduce:** **B1-d**: Can this part of the [story/text] be described as: a definition, a description, an explanation, a conversation, an opinion, an argument, or a comparison? How do you know? (fiction, nonfiction) **B2-a**: Why does the author include paragraph ___? (fiction, nonfiction)
C: Making reader/text connections	**Continue all previous objectives; introduce:** **C1-b**: Make a personal connection. Show how something that happened in the story is like something that happened in your own life. (fiction) **C2-a**: Which part of the [story/article] do you think was *most* important? Use information from the [story/article] to explain why you chose that part. (fiction, nonfiction)
D: Examining content and structure	**Continue all previous objectives; introduce:** **D1-b**: Choose a simile and explain why the author chose that simile. (fiction, nonfiction) **D2-c**: Using information in the text, write a paragraph that could have appeared in ___'s journal after ___ occurred. (fiction, nonfiction) **D3-b**: How are your customs different from the customs described in this story? (fiction)

Third Grade	
A: Forming a general understanding	Continue all previous objectives.
B: Developing an interpretation	**Continue all previous objectives; introduce:** **B2-b**: Why did the author write a [poem/story/ informational article/nonfiction book] about this topic? (fiction, nonfiction)
C: Making reader/text connections	Continue all previous objectives.
D: Examining content and structure	**Continue all previous objectives; introduce:** **D1-c**: How did the author create humor in paragraph ___? (fiction) **D1-d**: Give an example of personification in paragraph _____. (fiction) **D2-b**: Imagine you are going to give a talk to your lass about _____. What two points would you be sure to include in your speech? (nonfiction) **D3-a**: How does the author/character show that ____ is important to him/her? (fiction, nonfiction)

So many books, so little time! It is easy to be overwhelmed by the quantity of books available for use with students of any developmental level. The number of picture books alone boggles the mind. How do you decide which books are best aligned with different comprehension objectives? This is a question I hear a lot. It's that age-old dilemma: Do we give a man a fish so he can eat for a day? Or do we teach him to fish so he can eat for a lifetime?

Many teachers are so busy with their day-to-day teaching responsibilities that they aren't much interested in fishing. "Just tell me what books to use," they plead. I can appreciate this. Under the best of circumstances, finding a great book to teach a particular objective can be a time-consuming task. I can't even count the number of hours I've sat cross-legged on the floors of various school libraries and bookstores looking for the perfect picture book for…whatever. The pile of rejects is always considerably taller than those I ultimately choose to use.

For teachers who want the quick fix, I've included a list of picture books accompanying each objective in Chapters 6 through 9. It's not a huge list for each objective, but the books are all available and they "work." I use them for model lessons that I demonstrate in classrooms at many grade levels. I have also included a bibliography at the end of the book that lists all books alphabetically, along with possible objectives matched to each text.

The problem with any bibliography, however, is that it is frozen in time. Five minutes after you finish it, there are new books available that didn't exist when you added the final resource to your list. Even the most current bibliography is never really up-to-date.

That is why "learning to fish" does have its advantages. Once you know what you're looking for, you are empowered to select your own really great books. I like to examine picture books from three different perspectives. First, I try to determine whether the book represents the qualities of good literature that I have come to respect over the years. Second, I think it is important to note whether the text meets the criteria for worthy multicultural literature. Finally, if I can satisfy both of these criteria, I then examine the book to decide if it is a good match for the comprehension objective I wish to teach.

Later in this book, as each comprehension objective is introduced, a section titled "Teaching Tips" provides hints for selecting texts matched to that particular objective. You will note that I look at three factors as I narrow my search for the perfect picture book: genre, author, and theme. Before turning to the individual objectives, however, take a look at the two rubrics that follow. These additional supports will guide your way as you seek and select the very best books.

Using the bibliographies in this book

The picture books listed for use with each objective are typically divided into two categories: those appropriate for the *primary* level and those best suited to the *intermediate* level. The levels are only approximate, and teachers should feel free to select books for any grade from either list to meet students' needs. Books that celebrate racial, cultural, or ethnic diversity are designated with a "+."

The books can be used for whole-class lessons, though they could also be read to small groups of children. In addition to reading the book aloud, *think aloud* as well. This means pausing your reading periodically, after each page or two, to describe your thinking orally. While you can think aloud about any strategy you are applying in order to gain meaning, focus especially on the evidence you are finding to meet the identified comprehension objective: *Right here on this page I am noticing the words the author is using to help me visualize how Alexander felt when his mom forgot to put dessert in his lunchbox.*

You will want to read several books aloud to students to model the way you read strategically to find different kinds of evidence and to let students practice their strategic reading, too. You will also want to discuss the books after reading to give students the opportunity to extend and revise their comprehension. The very last step in this process is written response—for those students who are ready to put their great answers on paper. All of this is explained in Chapters 3 through 5. Before moving to those chapters, however, take a look at the additional supports that follow: **Rubric for Identifying Great Picture Books** and **Rubric for Selecting Multicultural Literature**.

Additional supports

Rubric for Identifying Great Picture Books. By describing ten easy-to-identify criteria, the **Rubric for Identifying Great Picture Books** which follows will help you gauge whether the text you choose is, in general, a worthy piece of literature to share with your students. You probably look at many of these criteria already; you just haven't thought about them before in rubric form. Which criteria are most important to you from your teacher-perspective? Which are the most critical to your students from their kid point-of-view? Do you and your students look for the same qualities in a good book? How might this insight make a difference to the books you read aloud?

Rubric for Selecting Multicultural Literature. As teachers we know it is important to choose books with characters of different ethnicities and from different cultures. But beyond that, what are the criteria for a worthy multicultural book? These criteria are often subtle—or maybe we're just not used to analyzing children's books for their fair portrayal of all people and cultures. In either case, use this **Rubric for Selecting Multicultural Literature** to guide you, adding these twelve criteria to the factors you consider when choosing books for your classroom library or for reading aloud to children. How do some of *your* favorite books rate, keeping in mind *all* of these criteria?

Moving on

Armed with a good book and the objective you identified in the last chapter, you can now plan for the kind of instruction that will make learning come alive for your students. Find out how to craft great instruction in Chapter 3.

RUBRIC FOR IDENTIFYING GREAT PICTURE BOOKS

Criteria*	0	1	2
Complexity	Too simple or two complex	Just a few opportunities for critical thinking	Lends itself to multiple points of view
Content depth	Not enough information or content is too advanced	Covers topic adequately; could offer more elaboration	Precise content with details perfectly suited to level of students
Amount of text per page; length of book	There is too much to read on each page; the book is too long to hold students' interest.	The amount of text per page is about right; the book may be a little too long.	The amount of text is just right for students at this grade level; it can be read in a single session.
Multidimensional characters	Stereotypic characters or one-dimensional characters	One main character that is well developed	Two or more characters that are multidimensional
Interesting language	Words are boring; sentence structure is repetitive; or vocabulary is too advanced	There are some instances of interesting word choice	Language is rhythmic; many interesting words; varied sentence structure; evidence of voice

Criteria*	0	1	2
Visual appeal	The Illustrations are uninspired or provide visual overload.	The illustrations support the text in an appropriate though unimaginative way.	Graphics enhance the text with rich images or a sense of playfulness.
Opportunities for connections	Very limited opportunities for any kind of connection	There are plentiful opportunities for text-to-self connections.	In addition to text/self connections, there are parallels to other texts and the world.
Multicultural representation	Characters are all Caucasian or represent cultural or ethnic stereotypes.	There are multiple ethnicities represented, but characters do not reflect the special features of their culture.	The unique features of different cultures are featured through the development of characters and plot.
Significance of the theme	There is no special theme, message, or lesson beyond the plot events.	The author is sending a message, but it is a predictable one handled in a predictable way.	The author is sending an important message that is somewhat unique and handled sensitively.
Creative treatment of the topic	The text is so predictable that students quickly lose interest.	The text holds students' interest through humor or unique treatment of the topic.	Analogies and abstractions help students think about the topic in a new way.

* Note that the same criteria may be used at different grade levels, though a book that is rated favorably in terms of (for example) content depth and complexity for first graders may not rank as high if it is to be read to students in grade three.

RUBRIC FOR SELECTING MULTICULTURAL LITERATURE
(Including but not limited to: Native-American, Hispanic, Asian, African-American, Caribbean-American, Jewish, and Middle-Eastern cultures)

Criteria	0	1	2
The book fulfills the criteria of *all* good literature with interesting characters, a strong plot, a useful message, and beautiful language.	The book is poorly written. It wouldn't be a good choice under any circumstances—even if you were not looking for multicultural literature.	The book is interesting enough to children, though it doesn't really qualify as excellent literature. It may or may not feature different cultures.	This is a book you can't wait to share with your students. It is beautifully written with vibrant characters, an interesting plot, and a great message. It celebrates diversity, too.
The book reveals the way people of this culture live *today* (unless its intent is to provide a historical account).	The book is stuck in the past. The plot may hint at current issues, but stereotypes from the past prevail in terms of people's appearance and behavior.	There are no obvious disconnects between past and present—but there is little evidence of immersion in modern culture either.	The book actively shows people of different cultures fully engaged in activities of today's world.
The book reveals characters who are competent problem solvers, responding in positive ways to challenges.	The characters are depicted as inferior and incapable of meeting life's challenges; they elicit sympathy rather than pride or respect.	The characters of different cultures are mainly backdrop characters, not main characters. The plot does not revolve around their actions.	The characters of different cultures are people you admire. They make good decisions that impact their life and their world in a positive way.
The book lends itself to a discussion of how this culture influenced the world in a positive way.	There is no mention of cultural influence—or the influence is negative.	The book is *only* about the cultural contribution. It is accurate but exaggerated.	The book embeds cultural influence in an authentic way. It is not the sole purpose of the book.
The book provides examples of the values by which people of this culture live.	The values portrayed are sometimes negative and stereotypic.	The book does not really explore the values of a culture, although the characters are portrayed in a positive way.	In this book, it is easy to identify the values by which people live. Different values are celebrated for different cultures.
The book does <u>not</u> build up one culture at the expense of another (e.g., All Native Americans are good; White people are bad.)	Characters are portrayed as either all good or all bad to showcase the value of one particular culture.	The book features one culture in a positive way but does not feature any other culture.	The book portrays multiple cultures in a positive and realistic way.

Criteria	0	1	2
The book depicts women in contemporary roles.	Women are portrayed as "second-class citizens" with very traditional roles and gender bias.	Women are viewed in contemporary roles but are not central characters in the text—so you don't really see their strengths.	Women are portrayed as central characters, equal to men in intelligence, professional role, etc.
The book inspires students to want to learn more about this culture.	The text and the illustrations are dull and do little to inspire further reading about the culture.	The book is apt to catch the interest of a few students but will not motivate most students at this level to read more on the topic.	Both the text and the illustrations pique students' curiosity about the culture and inspire students to look for other books about the same culture.
The book includes words and phrases in the language native to this culture.	No words or phrases of the native language are used.	Native words and phrases are used occasionally but in a mostly casual manner.	Native words and phrases are used to enhance the text's message.
The book's illustrations do not contain negative attitudes, offensive expressions, or stereotypes.	The illustrations portray typical stereotypes and set a negative tone for the book.	The illustrations are positive, but characters are "cartoonish" and sometimes act or look silly.	The illustrations are rich and provide additional insights into both the characters' values and the culture.
The book is historically accurate and does not oversimplify or exaggerate important historic events.	Some "facts" are inaccurate, or the entire text appears to be biased toward or against a particular culture.	The book appears to be accurate but minimizes or exaggerates particular historical events.	The book provides just the right details to convey historical events accurately and sensitively.

CHAPTER 3

Great Instruction

Great instruction increases the likelihood that *all* children will succeed. They may not achieve some arbitrary standard on a state assessment, but they will move forward, improving on their own past performance. What kind of instruction produces these positive gains? I am a staunch advocate of explicit, systematic instruction that gradually releases responsibility to students as they attain a suitable level of independence. This instructional design can be applied to teaching a skill or strategy in any curriculum area—in this case, to teaching comprehension objectives so that students can learn to produce high-quality oral and written responses.

Defining the components of explicit instruction

Explicit, systematic instruction that guides all students to independence on a specific learning task is comprised essentially of these components:

- An explanation
- Modeling
- Bridging
- Guided practice
- Independent application

As with all learning, it is important to consider that the learning *process* must culminate in a learning *product*, something that be measured. In this case, that product, measured through students' independent application, is a response to a comprehension question. That should happen first through assessing the quality of a student's *oral* response—and then, when developmentally appropriate, through a *written* response.

These lesson components should occur within both whole-class and small-group instruction. Whole-class instruction to introduce the objective should precede small-group instruction in a sequence similar to the one described in the following chart.

INTRODUCING A COMPREHENSION OBJECTIVE DURING WHOLE-CLASS INSTRUCTION

Lesson component	What does the teacher do?	What do the students do?
Explanation (3-5 minutes)	Teacher identifies the objective and explains to students how to identify evidence in the text for meeting the objective.	Students are able to articulate the lesson objective and identify criteria for meeting the objective once the teacher has explained it. Students may assist the teacher in establishing appropriate criteria.
Modeling (5 minutes)	The teacher models a few examples from the text, showing how to identify appropriate evidence by pausing to think aloud about her thinking process, linking the modeling to the explanation: *I notice here that the author is giving me lots of information about this character's feelings. That will help me decide what is important to this character.*	Students listen carefully to the teacher as she thinks aloud. After hearing a few examples modeled, they begin to offer their own insights into places in the text that provide evidence for meeting the objective: *I see something on this page that is important to this character...*
Bridging (7 minutes)	The teacher prompts students, actively eliciting more and more input from them to check who understands the objective and who is still experiencing problems: *Does anyone notice something about a character's feelings on this page?*	The students become more and more actively engaged in sharing their thinking with many children participating in the discussion.
Discussion (5 minutes)	After finishing reading the text (or portion of text), the teacher returns to the objective and asks students to respond to the question orally; the teacher gives *several* children the opportunity to respond, reinforcing good sentence structure. The teacher may ask other questions about the reading if time allows.	The students respond orally to the featured open-ended question and to other questions posed by the teacher. They respond in complete sentences, using some of the words in the sentence to frame their response. They follow the model provided by their teacher and peers.
Modeled written response and reflection (5 minutes)	Using a transparency or chart of the answer frame for the lesson objective, the teacher guides students in creating a shared response to the question. The teacher asks the students to read the completed answer with her orally. The teacher then reflects with students about the quality of the response: *What score would this answer receive?* The teacher concludes the lesson by helping students identify the steps they used to create their response in order to complete a similar response more independently in the future. Several children are given the opportunity to describe the sequence of steps.	The students volunteer ideas to fill in the answer frame, mindful of appropriate sentence structure. They join the teacher in re-reading their shared response chorally and evaluate its quality. When prompted by the teacher, students articulate the steps involved in producing a high-quality response to a similar question that they might be asked about another text in the future.

Especially in the lower primary grades, you may wish to continue to provide whole-class comprehension lessons that culminate in written response in order to reinforce the thinking necessary to answer a particular question. Most of the time, this will mean you are reading *to* children rather than having them read the text themselves since there are very few texts at the developmental level of *every* child in any class. Whole-class lessons where the teacher does the reading help students learn to *think* but do little to enhance *reading*.

An alternative to whole-class, follow-up lessons would be comprehension lessons during small-group instruction. The same lesson sequence would prevail. In either case, each time you teach a lesson reinforcing a particular objective, students should be held accountable for more and more independence in applying the process.

Follow-up lessons will take about 20 minutes, rather than the half hour needed for an introductory lesson. In follow-up lessons, the explanation should be more of a quick review (with more student talk than teacher talk). There should be no need for modeling or bridging as the teacher has already demonstrated to students how and where to find evidence in the text to support an objective, and students have been guided through the process with as much teacher-scaffolding as necessary.

Also in follow-up lessons, note that most of the time is devoted to *practicing*. Discussion following the reading remains the same. The big difference is that now the written response is produced by the *students*, not the *teacher*. It is a good idea to end the lesson with reflection. This helps students to assess their performance, solidifying what they did well, and determining what they can do a little better the next time.

These lessons may be repeated as often as necessary until students reach independence. "Independence" means that students see the question, understand immediately how to proceed with their reading to retrieve appropriate evidence to respond to the question, and then set about writing an answer that incorporates all of the steps needed to produce a high-quality response.

Be aware, however, that students may want to use the answer frame indefinitely unless you make a point of weaning them from it. As you begin to teach any comprehension objective, be prepared to tell students: *Today you may use the answer frame, and you may also use it tomorrow* (or any number of days you deem reasonable). *But by [Friday] I expect you to be able to write an answer to this question all by yourself on a blank piece of paper.* Now students know what standard they are expected to meet—and when. The framework for a follow-up lesson is described in the following chart.

REINFORCING A COMPREHENSION OBJECTIVE DURING WHOLE-CLASS OR SMALL-GROUP INSTRUCTION

Lesson component	What does the teacher do?	What do the students do?
Review of the objective (2 minutes)	The teacher asks students to identify the kind of evidence they should look for in their reading in order to respond to the objective (open-ended question) after reading.	Students confidently articulate the lesson objective and identify criteria for meeting the objective with very little prompting from the teacher.
Guided practice (7 minutes)	The teacher pauses her reading periodically (or students pause in their own reading) to think aloud about the evidence they have found in the text. The teacher may prompt students if they miss a key piece of evidence: *Is anyone noticing on this page how these two characters are different from each other?*	Students readily share their thinking aloud about places in the text where they have found important pieces of evidence related to the objective. They require less and less prompting over time, and begin to select their own places to pause to retrieve evidence.
Discussion (5 minutes)	The teacher facilitates a follow-up discussion that includes an oral response to the featured open-ended question (lesson objective).	Students articulate a well-structured oral response to the question that is accurate, logically organized, and suitably elaborated with specific evidence from the text. Several students respond orally.
Written response (7 minutes)	The teacher asks students to describe the steps needed to produce a good written response to the question and then distributes an answer frame to students who need this support. The teacher circulates among students, providing guidance as necessary. (After enough days of practice, the teacher will distribute a blank piece of paper rather than an answer frame for the written response.)	Students state the steps involved in writing a good response to the identified question when prompted by the teacher: *First.....Next.. Then...Finally.* They independently write their own answers. Note that in a whole-class lesson, they may not be able to quote directly from the text since they most likely will not have their own copy of the text in front of them.
Reflection (3-5 minutes)	The teacher asks a few volunteers to read their response aloud. Classmates are asked to identify strengths of the response, and aspects that could be improved.	Students read their own response aloud and/or listen to responses written by their peers. They identify strengths and weaknesses of the response based on a rubric or criteria chart (see Chapter 5, page 45).

The essence of explicit instruction

The previous chart provides a view-at-a-glance of *what* is involved in the explicit teaching of a comprehension objective that is measured by students' response to text. It does not, however, describe *how* to deliver each of these lesson components as meaningfully as possible. To that end, each lesson component is described in the rest of this chapter.

An explanation

Students need to know what kind of evidence to look for *as* they read in order to be able to answer the question *after* they read. This means that the teacher must explain up front, before reading, what kind of evidence or details to look for.

This is HUGE! When students tell you they don't know what to say in their response to a question, the main reason is that they didn't know what details to look for as they read. Unless teachers help students identify the *reading* strategy they should use to tap the evidence for a particular objective, all of the answer frames in the world will not help them to produce a solid answer.

Sometimes teachers think they can omit this part of instruction and begin their lesson with modeling. This doesn't work. The teacher may pause dutifully to model her thinking aloud, but students have no idea *how* she arrived at the decision to stop at that particular place or *why* that is an especially noteworthy piece of evidence. For example, are students trying to figure out how the author created humor in a text? It is not enough to stop and say, "Oh, look, here's a funny part."

Instead, the teacher needs to first help students decide what makes a text funny: Is it the exaggeration? Is it a play on words, or the sound of the language the author uses? Is it the visual image you get of the characters stuck in a tight situation? Clarifying what "counts" as evidence for meeting an objective gives students a way in. Now they know what to look for as they read.

Providing a good explanation is not as easy as it looks. As competent, adult readers, we almost instinctively know what to look for to understand the humor in a text or what kinds of things surprise us as we read, etc. But analyzing these strategies and breaking them down for children is another matter entirely. How do you really describe your thinking process for a particular reading task? At first, you will find yourself fumbling to find the right words. The good news, though, is that there is no single "correct" way to explain a comprehension objective. Any little hint or tip you can offer becomes one more new tool to make students' reading strategic.

All 40 templates in this book identify the reading strategy matched to that particular objective. This will be a good place to begin in offering students a suitable explanation.

Students can then retrieve the kind of evidence from the text that will help them respond knowledgeably to the comprehension question. The writing strategy is indicated as well so that students can represent their thinking meaningfully on paper.

Modeling

Good modeling is a beautiful thing to behold. It moves instruction from *telling* to *showing*, providing students with a tangible example of a practice implemented well: "Let me show you how *I* figure out the lesson this story teaches." "Watch me as I decide on the main idea of this article." When students see a strategy modeled, they are able to apply it themselves with greater competence and confidence.

Modeling can present challenges. First, make sure that the text you choose presents ample opportunities for modeling the strategy you want students to learn. If the story is heavy on action but limited in its treatment of characters, this would not be a good book to use for a focus on character development. If it is a personal narrative, there may not be much of a problem or conflict, so the text would not be a good one for teaching those story elements.

Something else to keep in mind when modeling is to always connect the point you are modeling back to the explanation of the strategy that you just gave to your students: "Remember when I told you that I would look for the setting right at the beginning of the story? Well, in this paragraph right here on page 1, the author is describing the setting." By linking the explanation to the example, the application of the strategy begins to take shape in students' minds.

Finally, do not let your modeling go on and on. During modeling, the teacher is highly engaged, stopping at key places in the text to describe her thinking and the evidence she has uncovered. The students, however, are mere spectators, witnessing this event from the sidelines but not really participating in it. They begin to lose interest, turning their attention instead to the child sitting alongside them on the carpet (little poke here, little poke there).

The most meaningful modeling is brief and has just enough examples to give kids a general sense of how this task looks when it is performed well. Then the teacher needs to begin to shift the responsibility for performing the task to the students. That's bridging!

Bridging

Many teachers are so focused on modeling that they nearly ignore bridging—the phase of instruction where students become accountable and where the teacher can see who understands the new strategy and who is still lost. In fact, within any explicit lesson, most of the minutes (10-15 minutes) should be devoted to bridging.

Begin bridging by first releasing just a little responsibility. For example, after modeling his thinking about evidence of character traits for two or three pages, a teacher might say, "This time when I find some words that Cinderella spoke, I will stop and ask what *you* think they show about what was important to her." Even later in the process, the teacher might ask students to decide for themselves places to stop to search for evidence of Cinderella's traits: her words, actions, thoughts, or appearance.

You'll want to check the progress of as many students as possible. With a whole-class (shared) lesson, you won't have a complete picture of every child's level of comfort with the new learning, but you should be able to answer one basic question: Do most students have a general sense of how to meet this objective, or are many of them still confused? If you conclude that you have too many "lost children," consider returning to the explanation or modeling phase to reinforce basic principles for everyone before attempting to move on.

If you find that most students "get it," but you have a few stragglers lagging behind, make a mental note to pull those children together for a small-group session to reteach the concept. In a small group, there will be more accountability and you can monitor students' progress more thoroughly.

You might even realize from your whole-class lesson that you have a group of students who are so competent with the new learning that they can skip some of the scheduled follow-up practice and move on to a more creative application of what they have learned.

In short, the bridging portion of the lesson is where teachers make decisions about differentiating the instruction that comes next. Without a significant amount of time devoted to bridging, it is impossible to teach diagnostically, to take the information we gleaned about our students today, to plan what we will teach them tomorrow.

Guided practice

Repeated practice is necessary not just for mastery of an objective, but for achieving independence with it. Keep in mind, however, that the old adage, "Practice makes perfect," is only partly true. Teachers beware: Practice without instruction does not make perfect; it only reinforces bad habits.

"Comprehension instruction" in some classrooms means packets of questions stapled together that students must answer every day—lots and lots of questions. This is the "more is better" approach and it doesn't work. In fact, it backfires. Students who must crank out page after page of answers to comprehension questions develop a kind of numbness to the entire process. With ten or more answers to write each day, their goal is not about getting to excellence, but just getting done. They don't care whether they write a well-elaborated response—or a sentence fragment—as long as there is *something* written under each question.

So what kind of practice makes sense? Begin teaching response to text first at the oral level. This will provide a general sense of "who understands what." Require just a few (even one is okay) written answers each day, and *teach* students how to respond so they recognize the criteria for a great answer. They will need a lot of support at first. On the first day, explain the criteria noted on the template for a good answer. Then model it by creating together a response that meets these criteria using a text identified in the bibliography or another of your own choosing.

At the early primary level, you will want to reproduce the templates in this book on chart paper and write the answers with your whole class as shared responses. Kindergarteners and first graders may be too young to write out lengthy answers right now. But they are definitely not too young to develop the thinking processes that will serve them well later on when they *can* read and write on their own.

Even with older students, when you first introduce an objective, you might want students to write a response using the exact text you used in your model. Of course (hopefully?), their answer will look a lot like yours. But remember that this is only the first day. Remind students that tomorrow you will not provide such a handy-dandy model; they will need to think about the criteria and write their responses themselves. So as they are writing their responses today, they should think about what is still confusing or troublesome so they can get their questions answered. This is how we lead students to independence.

Moving toward independence

When you first introduce written response to primary-grade children, struggling readers, and English language learners, it is fine to read a picture book (or another text) aloud to the whole class and use that to write a "class response." However, older students should transition to reading a text at a developmentally appropriate level *by themselves* and should respond *by themselves* to get an accurate measure of their performance. Teachers sometimes equate a student's capacity to write a good response to a question for a text that has been meticulously taught with his capacity to produce a response to a comparable question from a text that the student is reading himself for the very first time.

When the scores don't match, the teacher wonders, "What happened? James did so well on this question when we worked on it in class…" Without releasing responsibility all the way to independence, we can never count on students to apply what we think we have taught them. If we want to be able to say to our students with conviction, "That's a GREAT answer!" we must persevere until the strategies for reading and writing have become automatic and a blank piece of paper has taken the place of the answer frame with its scaffolded sentence starters.

Additional support: A lesson-planning template

The following lesson-planning template, **Choosing An Objective and Teaching It Explicitly**, offers teachers a format for embedding all of the essential components of explicit instruction into a whole-class comprehension lesson that focuses on written response. An example of a completed lesson-planning template is also provided to model the application of these best teaching practices.

Moving on

Explicit instruction that gradually releases responsibility to students looks very tidy. You move through its various stages step-by-step and in the end, students have mastered the strategy or skill that you set out to teach them. When the strategy is response to literature, however, we need to acknowledge that good written response is also a function of good oral response. Although we have already made a case for the importance of oral response in comprehension lessons, this is so critical that we need a clear understanding of exactly how to maximize its effectiveness. So before we examine what makes a great written answer, we need to consider what makes a great discussion. Chapter 4 offers some insights into how to get the most from classroom literature discussions.

CHOOSING AN OBJECTIVE AND TEACHING IT EXPLICITLY

Choose an objective:
(Identify an objective that is important for students at this developmental level.)

Choose your text:
(Identify a text that is well suited to this objective.)

How will you make the reading strategic?
(What tips or hints can you offer to students so they will know what evidence to look for in the text?)

Where can the strategy be applied in the text?
(Some of these applications should be <u>modeled by the teachers</u>, and some should be <u>practiced by the students</u>.)

Modeling

Practicing

How will you make the writing (or oral response) strategic?
(Can you give students a format to follow in order to write a well-organized response?)

CHOOSING AN OBJECTIVE AND TEACHING IT EXPLICITLY: COMPLETED EXAMPLE

Choose an objective:
(Identify an objective that is important for students at this developmental level.)

> **A2-b**: What is _____'s main problem in the story? Give details from the story to support your answer.

Choose your text:
(Identify a text that is well suited to this objective.)

> *Kitten's First Full Moon* by Kevin Henkes (This Caldecott Medal book is a very simple story that even kindergarten students can comprehend. It has an easy-to-identify problem with lots of details to support it.)

How will you make the reading strategic?
(What tips or hints can you offer to students so they will know what evidence to look for in the text?)

> 1. Look for the problem at the *beginning* of the story. (What is the main character having trouble doing?)
> 2. Find details that show this is a big problem.

Where can the strategy be applied in the text?
(Some of these applications should be <u>modeled by the teachers</u>, and some should be <u>practiced by the students</u>.)

Modeling
> p. 1: Kitten wanted her bowl of milk. She thought she saw it in the sky, but it was hard to reach. (This is the problem.)
> p. 4: When Kitten stretched her neck she got a bug on her tongue (no milk!)
> p. 8: When Kitten jumped to reach the milk, she tumbled and bumped her nose.

Practicing
> p. 11: Kitten chased the bowl of milk through the garden and by the pond, but she never got closer.
> p. 16: Kitten tried to climb a tree to reach the milk. She still couldn't reach it.
> p. 22: Kitten leaped into the pond to get her bowl of milk. She just got wet.

How will you make the writing (or oral response) strategic?
(Can you give students a format to follow in order to write a well-organized response?)
> 1. Tell about the big problem that this character was having.
> 2. Tell one place where the author *shows* this is a problem: What happens?
> 3. Try to find another place where the author *shows* you something about this problem.

See p. 66 of this book for an answer frame for this question.

CHAPTER 4
Great Discussions

Rethinking the reading process

If we thought about the parallels between the writing process and the reading process, we would better recognize the important role of oral discussion within our literacy instruction. With a few minor variations, the writing process is commonly regarded as a sequence of steps that moves from planning to drafting to revising to editing and, finally, to publishing.

We would do well to think of reading in much the same way. "Planning" is what occurs *before* reading as students activate their prior knowledge, make predictions, and set a purpose. As they read the text, they "draft" an initial understanding. For example, if they are reading a story, they identify the characters, problem, events, and solution. If they are reading a piece of nonfiction, they determine the big ideas and locate some of the supporting details.

Unfortunately, that is all we ask students to do much of the time before requiring them to "publish" their thinking about a text in the form of a written response. Meanwhile, what happened to "revision?" It is within the context of oral discussion that students revise their "first draft" comprehension of a text—as they listen to peers share their thinking and reshape their own, and as the teacher asks probing questions that encourage them to "go deeper" with their thinking. As they think out loud about a response, they get to hear that thinking—and that language—editing it in effect, before attempting to "publish" that thought on paper. Without the opportunity to revise and edit their thinking, it is amazing that students respond as well as they do to written questions.

What is the teacher's role in a good discussion about a book? What is the student's role? Even more basic, what does a good book discussion look like in a classroom?

What does a good book discussion look like in a classroom?

The composition of the group matters. For primary-grade students, struggling readers, and English language learners, most of these discussions will probably occur with a group of peers at their approximate reading level—if we expect students to *read* the texts they will discuss. It is certainly possible for other grouping configurations to occur as well, based on interest in a topic or a text, for instance.

Chapter 4 — Great Discussions   29

The size of the group matters, too. The best book discussions usually take place with just a few participants—not with an entire class. When too many students are in the mix, several of them will not participate (even if they are attentive). And it is impossible for the teacher to orchestrate the experience to get everyone engaged at a level that truly advances their thinking. The best book discussions generally include about five to eight students. If there are more than eight group members, some will not have the opportunity to fully participate, and it will also be difficult for the teacher to sufficiently monitor each student's performance. Fewer students (five or less) works well with struggling readers who need lots of coaching in order to stay actively engaged.

The children do more talking than the teacher. This is the best indicator of a productive book discussion, regardless of the composition of the group or the number of students involved. While this sounds easy enough, it is not the way most "discussions" play out in the classroom: The teacher asks a question. One child responds. If the answer is correct, the teacher moves on to the next question. Another child responds. And so the pattern continues. The teacher leads the charge determining who gets to speak at any given moment and deciding which answers are "correct."

Good book discussions help to create a community of learners where the teacher's role is to facilitate the conversation rather than direct it. In fact, if a teacher does her job well, she will become obsolete; the students will be able to carry out the discussion on their own. Until students reach that level of independence the teacher's job is to know when to clarify, model, coax, question—and especially, when to keep quiet.

Good book discussions have an almost palpable energy derived from every student's active involvement. Students are eager to participate because their thinking is respected, the environment is non-threatening, and there is no single "right answer." Their teacher is responsive to what students say so that each contribution builds on, challenges, or extends something that was stated previously. The following considerations may be helpful for teachers in maximizing the power of "book talk."

Facilitating a good book discussion: The teacher's role

Ask higher-level questions that are open-ended and elicit divergent responses. While the teacher has many responsibilities while facilitating a book discussion, his most important job is to ask good questions. When teachers ask a string of literal-level questions, there will not be much to discuss because there is a "correct" answer—and it is found right in the text. It doesn't make much sense to ask Diego if he agrees with Nigel about the outcome of the story because the author has already answered the question for both of them. For a discussion to happen, there needs to be clues in the text, but the meaning should be open to interpretation. Depending on your perspective, you might think one view—or another—is more justified. It's all open to debate—and that is where a good discussion begins. Consider beginning with the prompts below to get a good discussion going in *your* classroom—and to *keep* it going.

Note that different questions have different purposes.

- Initiate: Who would like to start us off by talking about _____?
- Explore: What can you tell me about _____?
- Add: Does anyone have another idea about _____?
- Disagree: Does anyone disagree with what _____ said about _____?
- Compare: How does _____ compare to _____?
- Connect: How does _____ relate to *your* life?
- Explain: Why did _____ happen?
- Take action: What would *you* do about _____?
- Cause/effect: If _____ occurred, what do you think might happen?
- Extend: Can you say more about _____?
- Prioritize: What do you think was *most* important about _____?
- Summarize: What have we learned so far about _____?
- Interpret: What is the author/character trying to show us here?
- Apply: Knowing _____, how would you _____?
- React: How did _____ make you feel?
- Clarify: What confused you about _____?
- Critique: What is the evidence for _____?
- Refocus: Are we still talking about our original idea?

Other teacher-facilitation skills

In addition to asking good questions, the teacher can promote high-level talk about text by attending to the following:

Begin with an objective that is clear, and post it so children can refer to it. Like everything else in literacy instruction, a good discussion is focused and has a clear objective. That makes it much easier to know when you are on-task or off-task. Making the objective visible to students by posting it on the board or overhead will help them stay focused, too.

Know the criteria for meeting the objective and explain the criteria to students. Each of the response templates in this book offers both a reading strategy and a writing strategy. The writing strategy describes the criteria for meeting that objective in *writing*. However, the same criteria could be applied to *oral* response. Teach children that their responses will be stronger if they think about the way they organize their answer and the kinds of details they add.

Use words and vocabulary that children can understand—but that also stretch their thinking. There is a fine line between making learning meaningful with familiar words and concepts and pushing students beyond their comfort zone to learn new academic language. The bottom line is that children need to understand the question in order to respond to it. Still, teachers can push a little to encourage deeper thinking: "Tell me more about…" "What evidence in the text suggests that you are right about…?" By explaining and defending their thinking, students will find the words to talk meaningfully about what they read.

Model the kinds of discussion behaviors you want your students to emulate. Show your students how *you* pick up on a point made by a member of the group and integrate your statement with the one just made: "The picture in my mind was almost like Noah's except that…" Then point out to students what you have done: "Did you notice how I listened to what Noah said and used that as a way to get into the conversation, connecting my idea to his?" You try to do that, too." Provide feedback to students when they succeed in demonstrating good discussion behaviors: "Nice job, Derrick. I love how you used what Meryl said to think of a new question to ask about this chapter."

Remember "wait time" in order to encourage participation. Resist the urge to call on the first student whose hand flies into the air after you ask a question. Typically, that child will be the first one to respond *every* time. When you wait five or six seconds before calling on a student, more children will have been able to process the question and will raise their hands. You also send the message that *everyone* needs to think about this question, not just the quickest thinkers in the group. Above all, never identify the student you want to answer a question before posing the question to the whole class. If you do, only that one student will be accountable to thinking about the response.

Don't answer your own question—or repeat or paraphrase students' responses. These techniques send the message to students that they can basically sit back; you will do the work for them. If they wait long enough before responding, you will get tired of the wait and jump in with the answer yourself. Likewise, they don't have to tune in to their peers as they respond because you will restate the answer afterward and probably rephrase it in language that is clearer and easier to comprehend.

Encourage students to talk to each other, not just to you. One of the noble goals of a classroom book discussion is to make it look and feel like a conversation that is *not* happening in school. Once students adjust to the conversational flow, they will begin to see that they don't always have to "follow the rules." For example, they don't really have to raise their hand in order to talk; they look for their opening and seize the moment (respectfully, of course). Furthermore, they don't need the teacher's "permission" to speak; they can decide for themselves when they want to say something, responding thoughtfully to other group members.

Find strategies to cope with students who try to dominate a discussion. You understand how important it is for *all* voices to be heard during a book discussion—or any discussion. However, every class has one or two students who want an abundance of "air time," thus silencing the voices of some of their quieter, more timid peers. (Even in my graduate classes this is an issue—with lots of sideways glances and eye-rolling from classmates who quickly lose patience with these overzealous talkers.) Some teachers use a system with "chips" that students "cash in" each time they speak. When you're out of chips, you're out of air time.

Find strategies to get reticent children to respond. These kids are the polar opposites of the students described above; they *never* participate—even when they know the answer, even when they are in a small group with little risk involved. These students could benefit from "chips," too: "Today I am giving you two chips, Tomás. That means you need to add something to our discussion two times."

Attend to nonverbal signals. Recognize the look of anticipation in a student's eyes, or the hesitant little hand that wants to respond—but can't quite find the courage. Watch your own nonverbal cues, too. Do your eyes show disapproval? Do you appear impatient or bored as students are responding? Show speakers that they have your full attention when they are talking. And smile.

Avoid "problem" questions. Some questions head straight for a dead-end, requiring only a *yes* or *no* response. Other times teachers develop a "formula" for questions which they don't recognize, but their students see right away: "Is the answer A or B?" "B" is almost always the answer—a hot tip for students who don't want the aggravation of having to actually *think* before answering. Also watch out for fuzzy questions. Sometimes teachers phrase questions in a way that even I can't understand. No wonder they get blank stares instead of good responses from students.

Participating in a book discussion: The student's role

Although the teacher has many responsibilities in helping a book discussion to take shape, it is the students who should be doing most of the work. First, they should arrive at the discussion carefully prepared. This means that they have completed any assigned tasks: read required pages, affixed sticky notes as instructed to note evidence, answered a written question if that was assigned, etc. They should also arrive with their book in hand and assemble themselves and their materials as quickly as possible so that the discussion can begin promptly.

During the discussion, students should listen attentively to their peers. This means establishing and maintaining eye contact by tracking the speaker and demonstrating nonverbal cues that show openness and thoughtful consideration rather than disrespect or disinterest. Students who participate constructively in a conversation are always respectful of their peers, even when disagreeing.

Students should show interest throughout a discussion not just by being a good listener, but by contributing appropriately. A good discussant knows how and when to enter a conversation, how much talk is too much and how much is just right. A good participant does not need to be prodded by the teacher to say something. And the *best* participants not only contribute on a regular basis, but also make comments that are insightful and ask probing questions. Students who are good at discussing make a point of staying on the topic and recognize when their comments begin to drift a bit and how to get back on track.

Students who are good at discussing learn how to build off their peers' ideas with comments or further questions in order to keep the conversation going. You may hear them begin their response with sentence starters such as:

- I agree with that idea, but I'd like to add _____.
- I'd like to build on _____'s thinking.
- I don't completely agree with _____ about _____. I'm thinking that _____.
- What evidence from the [story] supports your thinking about _____?
- _____'s comment makes me wonder _____.
- I'd like to go back to the point that _____ made about _____.
- I think we're getting off track. Let's stay focused on _____.
- My opinion [or connection or other strategy application] is almost like _____'s except that _____.

Prompts such as these lead students to a deeper understanding of a text. Their thinking truly will change as a result of the conversation. In this way, discussion takes its rightful place in the reading process as an opportunity for revising comprehension. This is so important before students attempt to "publish" their thinking on paper. Additionally, if teachers post these response starters and model them, students will soon enough be able to run their own small-group discussions about text.

Additional support

The **Rubric for Examining Teachers' Expertise in Leading a Discussion** on page 36 provides a reference for teachers to reflect on the quality of the literature discussions they lead. As with the use of any rubric, look for patterns over time, rather than performance on one specific day.

The **Discussion Rubric** on page 38 provides a reference for teachers to reflect on the quality of their students' participation in a literature discussion.

Students can be taught to self-reflect using the criteria checklist, **How Am I Doing When I Participate in a Discussion?** on page 39.

The **Discussion Planner** on page 40 offers a simple format for planning literature discussions for either whole-class or small-group discussions. Note that there are spaces for two questions within each of the four thinking strands. Determining which questions are well matched to a text beforehand (and writing them down) will help the discussion flow better and assure that a broad range of questions is addressed over time. When we invent questions "on the go," we tend to ask the same questions over and over—and many of them are at a literal level. Be sure that one of the questions you discuss is the focus question that will be used later for written response. Students who lack confidence in their ability to produce worthy responses will feel empowered if their thinking has been validated during a discussion—before they are expected to put that thinking on paper.

Moving on

With everything in its place—the objectives, the books, the instructional design, and even the discussion—students should have the expertise to produce quality written responses to open-ended comprehension questions. Chapter 5 examines some of the fine points for teaching the art of written response to text.

RUBRIC FOR EXAMINING TEACHERS' EXPERTISE
IN LEADING A DISCUSSION

Criteria	0	1	2
The teacher has an objective for the discussion and makes the objective clear to students.	There is no objective; the discussion just drifts from one focus to another.	The teacher generally focuses the discussion on an objective but does not clarify it to students.	The teacher consistently organizes discussion around a clear objective and articulates the objective to students.
The teacher understands the criteria for meeting the discussion objective and explains these criteria to students.	The teacher does not seem to understand how to help students meet the discussion objective.	The criteria are more general than specific.	The teacher begins the discussion with a description of the criteria by which students will be assessed.
The teacher asks higher-level questions that are open-ended and elicit divergent responses.	The questions are almost all literal with a single right answer.	There is a mix of literal- and higher-level questions.	Questions are consistently open-ended and promote higher-level, divergent thinking.
The teacher uses words and vocabulary that children can understand—but that also stretch their thinking.	Students are more confused than enlightened by the teacher's use of words.	Students use the words but do not seem to grasp their full meaning; the teacher does not appear aware of students' lack of understanding.	The academic vocabulary is rich, but the teacher provides sufficient guidance.
The teacher models the kinds of discussion behaviors that students should emulate.	There is no modeling; the teacher just expects students to figure things out on their own.	The teacher may model but does not explain to students *how* to engage in similar actions.	The teacher models good discussion behaviors and points these out to students.
The teacher remembers "wait time" in order to encourage student participation.	The teacher calls on the first student to raise his hand.	Sometimes the teacher uses "wait time" effectively, but other times the pace is too fast.	The teacher always gives students the time to process a question before seeking a response.
The teacher does not answer her own question or repeat or paraphrase students' responses.	The teacher quickly answers her own question if she gets no response or an incorrect response.	The teacher sometimes paraphrases students' responses or answers her own questions.	The teacher knows that faulty questioning strategies will enable but not empower students.

Criteria	0	1	2
The teacher encourages students to talk to each other, not just to her.	The teacher controls the talk. She poses all of the questions and decides who will talk and when.	The students talk to each other, but most responses come back to the teacher for grounding.	The teacher actively works to get students talking to each other.
The teacher finds strategies to cope with students who try to dominate a discussion.	The teacher clearly allows some students to dominate the discussion.	The teacher is aware of domineering students but has trouble dealing with them.	The teacher (in a kind way) makes sure no student dominates the discussion.
The teacher finds strategies to get reticent children to respond.	The teacher doesn't do anything to get the quiet kids talking—or even engaged.	The teacher attempts to get quiet students involved but is often not successful.	The teacher (in a kind way) gets even the quiet children to respond.
The teacher attends to her own nonverbal signals and those of her students.	The teacher is oblivious to nonverbal cues from her students or herself.	The teacher is aware of the impact of nonverbal cues, but does not always attend to them.	The teacher consistently attends to her nonverbal behaviors and those of her students.
The teacher avoids "problem" questions.	Many answers are obvious; there are too many yes/no responses.	The wording of some questions is confusing.	The teacher words questions carefully to avoid problems.

DISCUSSION RUBRIC

Student: _____   Date: _____

	0	**1**	**2**
Demonstrates preparation for the discussion and understanding of the objective	Student does not appear to have read or understood the text; does not refer to specific textual details; references do not make sense	Generally engaged in the discussion and makes some reference to specific details in the text	Engaged in the discussion and cites specific, relevant references to the text
Listens attentively to peers	Does not pay attention to the speaker; off task or too focused on sharing own ideas	Generally focused on response of speaker; sometimes appears distracted	Shows genuine interest in peers' responses; tracks speaker
Willingly volunteers ideas but does not dominate discussion	Seldom participates; makes random comments that show poor understanding of the text	Sometimes contributes to discussion but contributions do not show much critical thinking; may try to participate too much	Consistently contributes insightful comments and ideas with good sense of how much talking is appropriate
Respects opinions of other group members	Interrupts frequently; becomes argumentative when disagreeing	Generally respectful but sometimes interrupts speaker or disagrees in a negative way	Waits until the previous speaker is finished; encourages and supports the opinions of others, even when disagreeing
Builds off of peers' ideas with comments or further questions in order to keep the conversation going	Follow-up comments have nothing to do with preceding conversation; never asks questions	Sometimes builds off of peers' responses with further comments or questions	Integrates past comments into own comments; extends ideas by posing additional questions or follows up on peers' comments
Rethinks opinion based on ideas of other group members	Emphatically defends own stance—in spite of conflicting evidence	Sometimes willing to change stance based on input from group members	Synthesizes information from multiple sources in order to develop more informed opinion

Areas of strength: _____

_____

Areas of need: _____

_____

HOW AM I DOING WHEN I PARTICIPATE IN A DISCUSSION?

Name: _____ **Date:** _____

Today we had a discussion about: _____

❏ I was prepared for this discussion. I did all the reading and thought about what I might say.

❏ I listened carefully to other people in my group. I looked at them while they were speaking and concentrated on what they were saying.

❏ I joined the discussion without my teacher asking me. I showed that I was interested. I gave other people the chance to talk, too.

❏ I was polite even when I disagreed. I didn't act like my answer was the only good answer.

❏ I connected my response to another speaker's response in order to keep the conversation going. I said things like, "My opinion is almost the same as Tim's except…"

❏ I was open-minded. I was willing to change my opinion if someone else had a really great idea.

My best moment in this discussion was when: _____
_____.

When I am participating in a discussion, I need to get better at: _____
_____.

DISCUSSION PLANNER

A. Forming a general understanding

    1.

    2.

B. Developing an interpretation

    1.

    2.

C. Connecting and reacting

    1.

    2.

D. Structure and content

    1.

    2.

CHAPTER 5

Great Answers

Teaching tips for responding to specific comprehension questions will be addressed in Chapters 6 through 9. However, there are a few considerations that apply to *all* written responses, and those are described here.

What makes an answer great?

A great answer to a reading comprehension question *always* references the text with *specific* examples or details. The biggest reason for lost score points for open-ended questions is that students don't go back to the text to find the proof that supports their opinion. They may offer some general support, but they do not take the time to identify and write down the exact information that *shows* what they mean. The most unfortunate part of this is that you can often tell that students really *know* the answer; they simply choose not to record what they know.

To resolve this problem, repeat over and over the importance of "proving it in the text." Make a transparency of a response that lacks specific evidence and share it with the class (without the student's name, of course). Ask the class to determine why the response misses the mark, and invite students to suggest what would make the answer stronger. The irony is that when they are clear about the criteria, students are often harder on themselves than we are. Be sure to point out that some questions request "at least two pieces of evidence." In this case, evaluate their responses according to this more stringent standard.

A great answer is neither too long nor too short. "Longer" is not really better (but answers that are very brief may not have enough elaboration). Some students think that the more they write, the better their answer will be. This thinking is misguided for a couple of reasons: Answers that are longer than necessary often become redundant, or go off track. As teachers we've all been in the situation of sifting through lengthy responses with one basic idea repeated five different ways, or trying to find the central idea in a response that begins appropriately but then veers in several different directions with personal connections or editorial asides that distract us from the focus of the question. We sigh because it takes us so long to read these answers. And that's the second problem with "too-long" responses; it takes the student a long time to write them, too, time that could have been used more productively moving on to the next question.

Help students understand that quality responses include the information that is requested—and that is *all*. The answer frames will guide them. It almost always comes down to this:

- Use words from the question to create a topic sentence with your basic answer.
- Provide at least one piece of evidence (two pieces would be better) to prove your answer.
- When you have provided all the information requested, you are DONE.

In fact, I call this "get-the-job-done" writing. Unlike other genres of writing like stories and essays, we don't need to worry about entertaining beginnings and beautiful language. We only need to worry about demonstrating competence with the objective.

A great answer on an assessment will not serve you well unless you answer *all* of the questions. The problem here is that some children are quick to announce that they "don't have anything to say" for some questions. For example, if students are asked to think of two questions they would like to ask the author that were not answered in an article about whales, some student may announce, "There's nothing else I want to know about whales." They shrug and move on to the next question. Leaving answers blank is a VERY BAD IDEA because no response = no score.

Try to impress on students through many repetitions that, whatever it takes, they need to write *something*. Most written responses are scored on a scale. Even if the student doesn't receive full credit, perhaps she will receive a point or two. Those partial points add up and do boost scores, if only just a little. With solid teaching of comprehension objectives, students will feel more confident about how to approach different questions and they will be less likely to give up without trying.

A great answer is developed as a result of knowing what kind of evidence to look for as you read. Locating the right evidence is the lynchpin in the entire response process! When students tell you they don't know what to say in their response to a question, the main reason is that they didn't know what to look for as they read. Unless teachers help students identify the *reading* strategy they should use to tap the evidence for a particular objective, it will be impossible to produce a good response to that question, whether oral or written.

The solution to this problem is easy to identify, but teachers sometimes have a hard time implementing it. Teachers need to explain to students what "counts" as evidence for meeting an objective. They then need to model where they find that evidence in the text and, toward the end of the lesson, give students the opportunity to locate some of that evidence for themselves. In other words, in a shared lesson, teachers should not read an entire text as they would conduct a read-aloud. They should pause and note, "I'm noticing right here that [the character] is acting in a way that shows he is *kind*." "I'm figuring out that the problem in this story is…" Later, in the same text, the teacher should encourage the students to retrieve such evidence for an objective on their own. Note that for every comprehension objective in this book, the response template includes the *reading* strategy as well as the *writing* strategy.

A great answer must first of all be *accurate.* I know this sounds so obvious that it barely deserves mentioning. However, I've seen lots of written responses that are more fiction than fact. Some students, even young ones, are very good at making an answer sound plausible and quite "official," although it is just plain wrong. In response to a question about Goldilocks' misbehavior in the Bears' house, Jenna, a second grader, wrote: "Goldilocks broke Mama Bear's necklace when she tried it on." This was a clearly stated, specific detail that might have earned Jenna full credit—if this had actually happened in the story!

Remember, if an answer is not accurate, it doesn't matter whether or not it is well elaborated. That is why it is so important for the teacher to read the text, too.

A great answer is well organized, well elaborated, and fluent enough to be read without missing the meaning. Young children and older struggling readers often write their thoughts in a random fashion, just as they enter their mind. There is no logic to their sequence of ideas and they sometimes make the assumption that if an idea is in their head, it must also be in the head of their reader—thus eliminating the need for elaboration.

This is where the answer frames are especially helpful! Teach children that good readers and writers think about the order in which they tell their information. First comes the "big idea" statement which uses some words from the question. Then come the details that support the big idea. Point out that all good answers are organized in this fashion.

A great answer can be supported by the use of an answer frame at the beginning of the learning process; the goal is to eliminate the need for graphic support as soon as possible. Sometimes teachers approach me during a workshop unhappy that their students continue to rely on the answer frames I have provided them to write their responses. "Why do you think that happens?" I always ask them in return. The truth is that students continue to ask for the answer frames because teachers continue to offer them.

I remind teachers, "You need to make it clear on the first day you teach an objective that the answer frame will be useful *now* as students are learning to respond to a particular question. But everyone will be expected to write an answer without the frame by [pick a day]." Reinforce daily that students should be paying attention to how to organize their answer without the use of the frame because soon they will be expected to write their answer on a plain piece of paper.

The rubric at the end of this chapter will help teachers assess students' written (and oral) responses based on four criteria: accuracy, organization, elaboration, and fluency. A simple criteria chart is also provided for students' use so they can reflect on their own responses.

Moving on

Having read and reflected on the information in these five brief chapters, you are now ready to move on to the second part of this book—the tips, texts, and templates you will need to teach each of the comprehension objectives as effectively as possible.

RUBRIC FOR ASSESSING STUDENTS' ORAL AND WRITTEN RESPONSE
TO COMPREHENSION QUESTIONS

Name: _____ Date: _____

Question: _____

	0 Beginning	1 Developing	2 Accomplished
Accuracy	The answer is clearly inaccurate and is well below the range of developmental-level expectations. It does not indicate that the student has constructed basic meaning from the text, either as explicitly-stated information or as inferred relationships among ideas. The answer may point to problems that go deeper than comprehension—perhaps insufficient word-identification skills.	The answer is partially accurate. It shows some confusion about events or information described in the text, and inferences may be "far fetched" or not tied directly to the content of the reading.	The answer is completely accurate. It is clearly based on events in the text that really happened, correctly represents factual information, and formulates reasonable inferences.
Organization	The answer has no organizational framework and is well below the range of grade-level expectations. It may be too sparse to provide a sense of organization; it may be very long and repetitive, saying the same thing over and over in a variety of ways; or it may be largely incoherent with no sense of direction.	The answer is marginally organized. It may begin in a logical fashion, but loses its focus, or the parts may all be present but are not well-sequenced.	The answer is logically organized. It follows the steps specified in the response criteria or uses another sequential structure that makes sense to the reader.
Thoroughness	The answer is vague and/or irrelevant and is well below the range of grade-level expectations. It may be so general, far fetched, or loosely tied to the text that it is hard to tell whether the student has even read the text.	The answer is more general than specific. It contains some details and elaboration, but the student has missed or has neglected to include enough evidence from the text to sufficiently support a general statement or main idea.	The answer is thorough according to grade-level expectations. It meets all criteria for details and elaboration specified for the response to a particular question. The details show a close, careful reading of the text.
Fluency	The answer is nearly incomprehensible because of written language deficits and is well below the range of grade-level expectations. It shows extreme lack of skill in communicating ideas in writing and may signal the need for interventions beyond the scope of written-response instructional supports.	The answer sounds somewhat "choppy." It is generally able to be read and understood but may show more carelessness or lack of proficiency in the use of grammar, usage, writing conventions, vocabulary, and language structure than is appropriate for a student at this grade level.	The answer flows smoothly. It demonstrates grade-level-appropriate competence with grammar, usage, writing conventions, vocabulary, and language structure.

Greatest strength: _____

Next steps: _____

HOW AM I DOING ON WRITTEN RESPONSE?

Name: _____   **Date:** _____

Question: _____

I think my score on this question would be _____

❏   My answer is <u>correct</u>. The information came right from what I read.

❏   My answer is <u>organized</u>. It makes sense when I read it. It has a good order.

❏   My answer has plenty of <u>details</u>. It has examples or other evidence from the text.

❏   My answer is <u>written</u> so people can read it easily. I didn't leave words out. I tried to spell carefully. I remembered capitals and periods.

The best thing about my answer is _____

_____.

I still need to work on _____

_____.

PART 2:
TIPS, TEXTS, AND TEMPLATES FOR APPROACHING READING-COMPREHENSION OBJECTIVES

CHAPTER 6
Forming a General Understanding

Although the objectives within the "A" strand represent *general* understanding of a narrative or expository text, many of these objectives require more than literal-level thinking. In order to determine the lesson, theme, main idea, or a new title, students have to synthesize or put together details from the text and decide what these story elements *mean* beyond the story itself. Making a prediction about what might happen next also demands inferential thinking. Other objectives in this strand are more straightforward. They ask students to comprehend characters, problems, and solutions, but the answers can be found in words taken directly from the text. Additionally, to master the art of thinking at a "general understanding" level, students need to summarize text.

Objectives addressed in this book for *Strand A: Forming a General Understanding* are listed below. As with the strands that follow, other objectives could be included in each area, but for primary-grade students, struggling readers, or English language learners, these objectives are good places to begin and are generic enough to be applied to any fiction or nonfiction text.

The "A" strand: Forming a general understanding	
A1: Main idea and theme	**A1-a**: What lesson does _____ learn in this story? (fiction) **A1-b**: What is the theme of this story? (fiction) **A1-c**: What is this book/article mainly about? (nonfiction) **A1-d**: What would be another good title for this story/ text? (fiction, nonfiction)
A2: Characters, problem/solution, setting	**A2-a**: Using information in the story, write a brief description of how _____ felt when _____. (fiction) **A2-b**: What is _____'s main problem in the story? Give details from the story to support your answer. (fiction) **A2-c**: How did _____ solve his/her problem? Give details from the story to support your answer. (fiction) **A2-d**: How did _____ change from the beginning to the end of the story? (fiction) **A2-e**: What is the setting of this story? Give details from the story to support your answer. (fiction)
A3: Summarizing	**A3-a**: Briefly summarize this story. (fiction) **A3-b**: Summarize the main things that happened in this [book]. (fiction, nonfiction) **A3-c**: Briefly summarize this article/informational text. (nonfiction)
A4: Predicting	**A4-a**: Predict what will happen next in this story. (fiction) **A4-b**: If the author added another paragraph to the end of the story (or article), it would most likely tell about _____. Use information from the story (or article) to support your answer. (fiction, nonfiction)

A1-a: What lesson does _____ learn in this story? (fiction)

Grade level: K-3

Teaching tips: Identifying the lesson a character learned in a story is a fairly easy concept, even for young students. For example, after listening to the story *Stand Tall, Molly Lou Melon,* children are quick to say, "Ronald Durkin was a bully. He learned it is not nice to be a bully." After hearing *The Rainbow Fish*, they might tell you, "The Rainbow Fish learned that if you want to have friends, you have to be kind to everyone." Because young children see issues as right or wrong, they readily identify "good" and "bad" characters and can tell you what the "bad character" did that was naughty.

Texts in which a "bad" character learns to change his or her behavior from the beginning to the end of a story are good choices for teaching this objective. Older primary students are also able to identify the lesson in texts where good behavior is rewarded. An example of such a story is *The Lion Who Wanted to Love.* In this story, a lion cub breaks with tradition and tries to get his mom to understand that he prefers loving and helping other jungle animals rather than fighting and dominating them. His mother does not approve. But later, his kindness is repaid when his friends return his many favors by saving his life in a time of need.

Texts for teaching the lesson learned

Primary
- *A Bad Case of Stripes* by David Shannon
- *Down the Road* by Alice Schertle+
- *Princess Penelope's Parrot* by Helen Lester
- *Stand Tall, Molly Lou Melon* by Patty Lovell
- *The Honest-to-Goodness Truth* by Patricia C. McKissack
- *The Lion Who Wanted to Love* by Giles Andreae and David Wojtowycz
- *The Rainbow Fish* by Marcus Pfister
- *Too Many Tamales* by Gary Soto+

Intermediate
- *Children of the Earth and Sky: Five Stories about Native American Children* by Stephen Krensky
- *Fables* by Arnold Lobel
- *Freedom School, Yes!* By Amy Littlesugar+
- *Melissa Parkington's Beautiful, Beautiful Hair* by Pat Brisson
- *Odd Boy Out: Young Albert Einstein* by Don Brown
- *Rosa* by Nikki Giovanni+
- *The Paperbag Princess* by Robert Munsch
- *The Quiltmaker's Gift* by Jeff Brumbeau
- *The Summer My Father was Ten* by Pat Brisson
- *When Marian Sang* by Pam Munoz Ryan+
- *Wings* by Christopher Myers

Name: _____ **Date:** _____

A1-a: What lesson does this story teach?

<u>Strategy for reading</u>
Look for someone who is badly behaved at the beginning of the story. Does the person change by the end of the story? Think about what that person learned from his or her bad behavior.

<u>Strategy for writing</u>
1. Tell what lesson was learned.
2. Tell how the character was acting at the beginning of the story.
3. Tell how the character was acting at the end of the story.

The lesson in this story is _____
_____
_____.

At the beginning of the story_____
_____
_____.

At the end of the story_____
_____
_____.

A1-b: What is the theme of this story? (fiction)

Grade level: 2-3

Teaching tips: Determining a theme is more difficult than identifying a lesson. It requires students to think abstractly, beyond the text itself, to identify a universal message. This is hard for young children. In order to teach this objective, select texts where the story is simple and the theme is obvious. You may want to ask students to identify the author's *message*, rather than the *theme*. Examples of texts with a simple, clear message might be *Leo the Late Bloomer*: Everyone "blooms" in his/her own time. *Tacky the Penguin* is another simple story with a message that young children can understand: It's okay to be yourself; it's good to be a creative thinker. Some questions I typically ask students when I want them to comprehend the theme of a text are, "Why do you think the author wrote this book?" "What do you think he or she wants us to think about?" "What do you understand a little better after reading this book?"

Fairy tales generally have a universal theme. So do myths and legends and many books of realistic fiction.

Texts for teaching the theme of the story

Primary
- *Big Al* by Andrew Clements
- Fairy tales
- *Keep Climbing, Girls* by Beah E. Richards+
- *Koala Lou* by Mem Fox
- *Leo the Late Bloomer* by Robert Kraus
- *Peppe the Lamplighter* by Elisa Bartone
- *Sister Anne's Hands* by Marybeth Lorbiecki+
- *Something Beautiful* by Sharon Dennis Wyeth+
- *Tacky the Penguin* by Helen Lester
- *The Land of Many Colors* by Klamath County YMCA Family Preschool+
- *Whoever You Are* by Mem Fox

Intermediate
- *Aunt Chip and the Great Triple Creek Dam Affair* by Patricia Polacco
- *Dream: A Tale of Wonder, Wisdom & Wishes* by Susan V. Bosak
- *Freedom Summer* by Deborah Wiles+
- *Hewitt Anderson's Great Big Life* by Jerdine Nolen
- *Tar Beach* by Faith Ringgold
- *The Other Side* by Jacqueline Woodson+
- *The Royal Bee* by Frances Park and Ginger Park+
- *The Three Questions* by Jon J. Muth

- *The Tree that Would Not Die* by Ellen Levine
- *Uncle Jed's Barbershop* by Margaree King Mitchell+
- *Weslandia* by Paul Fleishman

Name: _____ **Date:** _____

A1-b: What is the theme of this story?

<u>Strategy for reading</u>
As you read, think about the message the author is sending you. What does the author want you to know about life or about how people should act or treat each other? Look for details in the story that *show* the message the author is sending you.

<u>Strategy for writing</u>
1. Tell the theme (or message) of the story.
2. Tell one detail that *shows* the message the author was sending you.
3. Tell another detail that *shows* the author's message.

The theme of this story is _____

_____

_____ .

One way the author showed this was _____

_____

_____ .

Another way the author showed this was _____

_____

_____ .

A1-c: What is this book/article mainly about? (nonfiction)

Grade level: 1-3

Teaching tips: Although this objective falls within the "general understanding" strand, it is one of the most difficult to teach—at *any* grade level. Why is it so difficult? The main idea of a text is almost never stated directly; it is inferred from synthesizing all of the information presented in the passage. After teaching children (from a very young age) that they need to go back to the passage and "find the evidence," for a response, there is nothing specific they can retrieve there that will lead them directly to its main idea.

So how does a teacher approach this objective? One possibility is to begin with a picture and ask students to figure out the "big idea" (or main idea) that the picture represents. It can be a calendar picture depicting a scene: "The tall mountains look beautiful with the sun shining on them." It can be a photograph of a birthday party: "The children were having a great time eating birthday cake." Any picture will do! The important thing is to help children understand there are many details in the picture that *lead* them to the main idea—even though there are no words that *tell* them the main idea directly.

Another way to approach main idea is to use nonfiction text with subheadings. The easiest subheadings to use are ones that are stated as questions: "What was Martin Luther King's Dream?" or "What are cumulous clouds?" The information that follows answers that question. After reading the passage, can students answer the question posed in the subheading in a simple sentence? That is the main idea.

When the subheading is not presented as a question, help students convert it to a question themselves. A subheading labeled "Caring for a puppy" could become "How do you care for a puppy?" Again, the answer to that question, briefly stated, is the main idea.

Be sure students understand that if they have found the "real" main idea, they should be able to find some details to support it. The graphic organizer on page 58 may help children grasp the concept of main idea and supporting details.

Texts for teaching about main idea

Primary
- *Be My Neighbor* by Maya Ajmera & John Ivanko+
- *Bugs for Lunch* by Margery Facklam
- *Firefighters* by Christopher Mitten
- *George Washington: A Picture Book Biography* by James Cross Giblin
- *Kindergarten Kids* by Ellen B. Senisi
- *Ricardo's Day* by George Ancona+

Intermediate
- Books with subheadings
- *A River Ran Wild* by Lynne Cherry
- *If You Traveled West in a Covered Wagon* by Ellen Levine and other books in this series published by Scholastic are excellent resources for teaching main idea.
- *Immigrant Kids* by Russell Freedman
- *Journey to Ellis Island* by Carol Bierman
- *Lincoln: A Photobiography, The Wright Brothers,* and others by Russell Freedman
- *The Icky Bug Alphabet Book, The Ocean Alphabet Book, The Boat Alphabet Book,* and many others in this series by Jerry Palotta

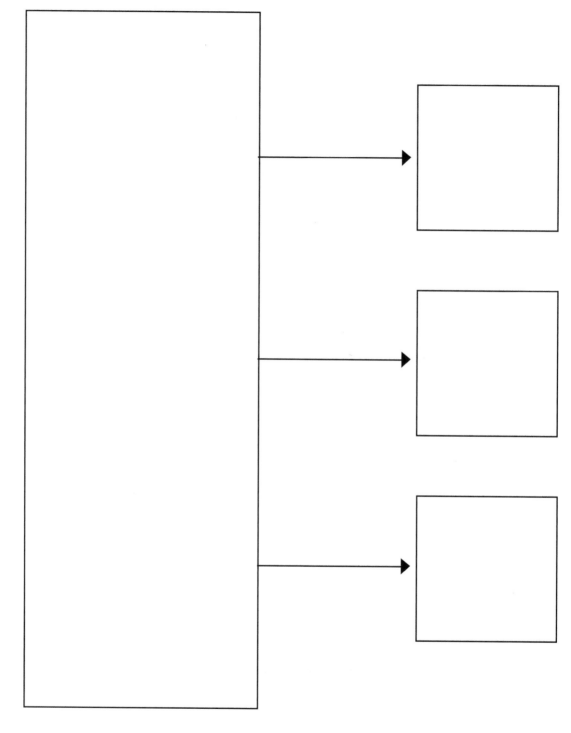

MAIN IDEA AND SUPPORT

That's a GREAT Answer!

Name: _____ **Date:** _____

A1-c: What is this book/article mainly about? (nonfiction)

<u>Strategy for reading</u>
As you read, stop every so often and think about what the author is talking about in that part of the text. When you are done reading, think of *one word or phrase* that describes what the reading is *mostly* about. Now turn that idea into a whole sentence. *That* is the main idea! If you have found the "real" main idea, you should be able to find some details that *show* that this is the main idea. Look for at least two details!

<u>Strategy for writing</u>
1. Tell what the main idea is.
2. Give one detail that shows how you know this is the main idea.
3. Give another detail that shows how you know this is the main idea.

The main idea is _____

_____

_____.

One detail that shows this is the main idea is: _____

_____

_____.

Another detail that shows this is the main idea is: _____

_____

_____.

A1-d: What would be another good title for this story/text? (fiction, nonfiction)

Grade level: 1-3

Teaching tips: Although there are many ways to determine a title for a text, a question that asks students to think of a title, or an alternate title, typically does so to assess their understanding of main idea: If a student comprehends the basic meaning of a text, choosing a title should be easy. With primary students, read them a story or poem without telling them the title. Then ask, "What would be a good title for this story (or poem)? For young children, choosing a name for a text that doesn't have a title is often easier than thinking up a new name for a title that already exists. For slightly older students, chapter books with chapters that are numbered but not titled are also good sources for inventing titles.

Another source I have used for finding new titles is the poetry of Jack Prelutsky. (Books include *The New Kid on the Block, A Pizza the Size of the Sun, Something Big has Been Here*, and others.) In many of Prelutsky's poems, the first line of the poem becomes the title as well. When children discover this, they recognize that such an approach is not very creative. They enjoy the challenge of "helping" Jack Prelutsky invent titles that are more alluring.

Texts for teaching how to find a new title (primary and intermediate)

- Poetry (especially poems by Jack Prelutsky)
- Individual chapters from a chapter books that are numbered but not titled

A1-d: What would be another good title for this story/text?

<u>Strategy for reading</u>
Think what the story/text is *mostly* about. The author won't come right out
and *tell* you what the story is mostly about; you will need to figure this out by
noticing the details. The title you choose should have something to do with the
main idea of the story or article.

<u>Strategy for writing</u>
1. Tell the new title that you have chosen.
2. Tell why you think this is a good title. (Your new title should connect to
    what the story/text is mostly about.)
3. Give an example from the text that shows *why* this is a good title.

Another good title for this [story/article] would be _____
_____.
This is a good title because this [story/article] is mainly about: _____
_____.
Here is a detail from the [story/article] that shows this: _____
_____
_____.

A2-a: Using information in the story, write a brief description of how _____ felt when _____. (fiction)

Grade level: K-3

Teaching tips: This is an easy objective for even early primary students to master. Young children are familiar with the concept of feelings, and they are able to articulate how a character would feel in a particular situation. Often, however, the feelings they ascribe to a character are those boring, tired "feeling" words we hear all the time: *happy* and *sad*. If we want children to describe feelings more precisely, we need to introduce them to more specific language: *thrilled* instead of *happy*, *sorrowful* as an alternative to *sad*. I encourage teachers to create a word wall of feeling words and then add to it as characters are discussed and their feelings are identified. One genre of text that commonly features feelings is personal narrative. Since characters are describing themselves or people who are near and dear to them, feelings often play a big role.

Texts for teaching about a character's feelings

Primary
- *Boomer's Big Surprise* by Constance McGeorge
- *Chrysanthemum* by Kevin Henkes
- *Corduroy* by Don Freeman
- *Do Like Kyla* by Angela Johnson+
- *Fireflies* by Julie Brinckloe
- *Kitten's First Full Moon* by Kevin Henkes
- *My Rotten Redheaded Older Brother* by Patricia Polacco
- *Wemberly Worried* by Kevin Henkes
- *Whistle for Willie* by Ezra Jack Keats+

Intermediate
- *Coming On Home Soon* by Jacqueline Woodson+
- *Faraway Home* by Jane Kurtz
- *Mama Loves Me from Away* by Pat Brisson
- *Meet Danitra Brown* by Nikki Grimes+
- *Minty: A Story of Young Harriet Tubman* by Alan Schroeder+
- *Nettie's Trip South* by Ann Turner
- *One Green Apple* by Eve Bunting
- *Some Frog!* by Eve Bunting
- *Star of Fear, Star of Hope* by Jo Hoestlandt
- *Thank You, Mr. Falker* by Patricia Polacco
- *The Honest-to-Goodness Truth* by Patricia C. McKissack+
- *The Memory String* by Eve Bunting
- *When Marian Sang* by Pam Munoz Ryan+

Name: _____ **Date:** _____

A2-a: Using information in the story, write a brief description of how
           _____ felt when _____.

<u>Strategy for reading</u>
What event in the story does the question ask you to look for? Be sure to read
that part very carefully. How does this event make the character feel? Look for
things the character *says* or *thinks* or *does* to give you some clues. Think of a
word to describe this feeling.

<u>Strategy for writing</u>
    1. Name the character's *feeling*.
    2. Tell one way the character showed this feeling.
    3. Tell another way the character showed this feeling.

When _____happened,
                  Event
_____felt _____.
      Character   Feeling
This character showed this by _____

_____

_____.

This character also showed this by _____

_____

_____.

> **A2-b:** What is _____'s main problem in the story? Give details from the story to support your answer. (fiction)
>
> **A2-c:** How did ____ solve the problem? Give details from the story to support your answer. (fiction)

Grade level: 1-3

Teaching tips: Identifying the main problem in a story and then finding its solution can be difficult. Children sometimes think that the event that occurs right before the turning point is the problem. They don't realize that the problem is the situation that initiates the action in the first place. They need to realize that the *main* problem is most likely revealed close to the beginning of the story. The solution occurs at the *end*. The main problem is the situation that eventually gets resolved; students should look for this link. Teachers can make the task of identifying the story's problem and solution easier for children by selecting texts that have a clearly defined problem that is *actively solved* by the main character.

In some stories, the problem gets resolved, but the main is not responsible for the solution; the solution just "happens" or someone else does the solving. An example of a book where the main character does not actively *do* anything to solve his problem is *Leo the Late Bloomer* by Robert Kraus. Leo "bloomed" because he simply grew up. In another example, *Kitten's First Full Moon* by Kevin Henkes, the bowl of milk that the kitten desires just shows up on the doorstep.

Teachers need to be especially sure that they do not ask children to identify the problem in a text where there isn't really a problem. Many personal narratives or memoir texts do not have clearly delineated problems. An example of a personal narrative without an identifiable problem might be *Mama, Where are You From?* by Marie Bradby. This book depicts a variety of events in Mama's life, but none would qualify as a problem; there is nothing to resolve.

Texts for teaching problem/solution

Primary
- *A Chair for My Mother* by Vera B. Williams
- *Dandelion* by Don Freeman
- *Hooway for Wodney Wat* by Helen Lester
- *Ira Sleeps Over* by Bernard Waber
- *Joseph had a Little Overcoat* by Simms Taback
- *Officer Buckle and Gloria* by Peggy Rathmann
- *The Kissing Hand* by Audrey Penn
- *The Little Engine that Could* by Watty Piper
- *The Story of Jumping Mouse* by John Steptoe

- *Umbrella* by Taro Yashima
- *Whistle for Willie* by Ezra Jack Keats+

Intermediate
- *Keepers* by Jeri Hanel Watts and Felicia Marshall
- *The Bus Ride* by William Miller+
- *The Cats in Krasinski Square* by Karen Hesse+
- *The Other Side* by Jacqueline Woodson+
- *The Paperbag Princess* By Robert N. Munsch
- *The Quiltmaker's Gift* by Jeff Brumbeau
- *The Wretched Stone* by Chris Van Allsburg
- *The Yellow Star* by Carmen Agra Deedy+
- *Virgie Goes to School with Us Boys* by Elizabeth F. Howard+

Name: _____ **Date:** _____

A2-b: What was _____'s main problem in the story? Give details from the story to support your answer.

Strategy for reading
Look for the problem at the *beginning* of the story. What is the character having trouble doing? What isn't working out for him or her? Sometimes there are lots of *little* problems. Try to find the *biggest* problem that this character was facing. Find details that show this is the problem.

Strategy for writing
1. Tell about the big problem that this character was having.
2. Tell one place where the author *shows* this is a problem: What happens?
3. Try to find another place where the author *shows* you something about this problem.

This character's main problem was _____
_____.
This was a problem when _____
_____
_____.
Another time this was a problem was when _____
_____
_____.

**A2-c: How did _____ solve his or her problem? Give a detail from the
story to support your answer.**

Strategy for reading

At the *beginning* of the story, look for the problem. Make sure you know what
the problem is. Toward the *end* of the story, look for how the problem gets
solved. What did the character *do* to fix the problem? Who helped solve it?
How did everyone feel at the end?

Strategy for writing
 1. Tell how the problem got solved.
 2. Tell what the character *did* to solve the problem.
 3. You can add a sentence about how everyone felt at the end, too.

The problem in this story got solved when _____
_____.

Here is what happened to solve this problem: _____
_____
_____.

At the end of the story, everyone felt_____
_____
_____.

A2-d: How did _____ change from the beginning to the end of the story? (fiction)

Grade level: 1-3

Teaching tips: The most obvious problem when teaching this objective is that sometimes teachers ask students to identify a character who changes in a text when the character doesn't really change. An example of this would be Alexander in the story *Alexander and the Terrible, Horrible, No Good, Very Bad Day*. In this story, poor Alexander never manages to improve upon his very bad day. In order for young children to succeed with this objective, the change that a character undergoes has to be extreme and obvious, a total turnaround in behavior: At the beginning of the story, the character might be a mean bully; by the end, he has turned into a nice kid. An example of a text where the character changes dramatically is *The Rainbow Fish*. In order to *have* friends, Rainbow Fish discovers he must *be* a friend.

Primary-grade students are not likely to notice subtle differences in attitude that signify change in more sophisticated texts, though this would be very appropriate for intermediate grade students. Note as well that it is not always the main character who changes.

Texts for teaching about characters who change

Primary
- *I Hate English!* by Ellen Levine+
- *Leo the Late Bloomer* by Robert Kraus
- *Peppe the Lamplighter* by Elisa Bartone
- *Princess Penelope's Parrot* by Helen Lester
- *Rainbow Fish* by Marcus Pfister
- *Stand Tall, Molly Lou Melon* by Patty Lovell
- *The Honest-to-Goodness Truth* by Patricia C. McKissack+
- *The Lion Who Wanted to Love* by Giles Andreae and David Wojtowycz
- *When I was Little* by Jamie Lee Curtis

Intermediate
- *A Bad Case of Stripes* by David Shannon
- *Dream: A Tale of Wonder, Wisdom & Wishes* by Susan V. Bosak
- *Freedom School, Yes!* by Amy Littlesugar
- *Me, All Alone, at the End of the World* by M.T. Anderson
- *Melissa Parkington's Beautiful, Beautiful Hair* by Pat Brisson
- *My Rotten Redheaded Older Brother* by Patricia Polacco
- *She's Wearing a Dead Bird on her Head!* by Kathryn Lasky
- *The Memory String* by Eve Bunting
- *The Name Jar* by Yangsook Choi+

Name: _____ **Date:** _____

**A2-d: How did _____ change from the beginning to the end of
the story?**

Strategy for reading
Pay special attention to the way this character is acting at the beginning of
the story. Find places in the story where the author *shows* what this character
thinks at first. Read carefully to notice where the character's thinking changes.
How does this character act at the end of the story? Can you find the *first place*
in the story where the character shows this change? (It will probably be close to
the end of the story.)

Strategy for writing
1. Tell how the character acted or what he or she thought at the *beginning*
   of the story.
2. Tell how the character acted or what he or she thought at the *end* of the
   story.
3. Tell the *first thing* the character said or did that showed he or she
   changed.

At the beginning of the story, this character acted like _____

_____.

At the end of the story, this character acted like _____

_____.

Here is something that shows the character changed: _____

_____

_____.

A2-e: What is the setting of this story? Give details from the story to support your answer. (fiction)

Grade level: K-3

Teaching tips: Unlike the story elements of character, problem, and solution, the setting of a story is often neglected as an instructional focus. This is unfortunate because a deeper exploration of where and when a story takes place might enhance students' understanding of setting in their writing as well as in their reading.

Books that feature setting in an important way are not necessarily the same ones that feature a strong plot. For the setting to "grab" our youngest readers, the story needs to be *about* the setting. For example, look for books *about* the rainforest, books *about* the seashore, and books *about* the North Pole. When students get a bit older, multicultural picture books are great resources, where students can examine the illustrations as well as the words to determine important elements of the setting—and how it is similar to and different from their own real-life setting. Additionally, check picture-book biographies of people from history as well as historical fiction for the later primary grades, as maturing readers should be able to note features of a setting that existed in the past.

To support students' understanding of *setting,* be sure to select some books where *time*, not just *place*, is significant in deriving meaning from the text. A couple examples of texts where the time is a critical factor would be *The Bracelet* and *Baseball Saved Us.* Both are stories about life in Japanese internment camps following World War II. In addition to glimpsing life in these dreadful camps, students need to recognize the role of history in establishing them.

Texts for teaching about setting

Primary
- *All the Places to Love* by Patricia MacLachlan
- *Bigmama's* by Donald Crews
- *Mama Panya's Pancakes: A Village Tale from Kenya* by Mary and Rich Chamberlain+
- *The Bracelet* by Yoshiko Uchida
- *The Great Kapok Tree* by Lynne Cherry+
- *The Korean Cinderella* by Shirley Climo+
- *The Little Island* by Margaret Wise Brown
- *The Year I Didn't Go to School* by Giselle Potter+
- *When I was Young in the Mountains* by Cynthia Rylant

Intermediate

- *A River Ran Wild* by Lynne Cherry
- *Appalachia: The Voices of Sleeping Birds* by Cynthia Rylant
- *Baseball Saved Us* by Kn Mochizuki+
- *Brothers in Hope: The Story of the Lost Boys of Sudan* by Mary Williams+
- *Christmas in the Big House, Christmas in the Quarters* by Patricia C. McKissack and Fredrick McKissack+
- *Heroes* by Ken Mochizuki
- *Letting Swift River Go* by Jane Yolen
- *Long Night Moon* by Cynthia Rylant+
- *Mercedes and the Chocolate Pilot* by Margot Theis Raven+
- *My Freedom Trip: A Child's Escape from North Korea* by Frances Park and Ginger Park+
- *Owen and Mzee: The True Story of a Remarkable Friendship* by Isabella Hatkoff, Craig Hatkoff, and Dr. Paula Kahumbu
- *Sami and the Time of the Troubles* by Florence Parry Heide and Judith Heide Gilliland+
- *Scarecrow* by Cynthia Rylant
- *The Bracelet* by Yoshiko Uchida+
- *The Lotus Seed* by Sherry Garland+
- *The Royal Bee* by Frances Park and Ginger Park+

A2-e: What is the setting of this story? Give details from the story to support your answer.

<u>Strategy for reading</u>

Where a story takes place is called its *setting*. The author usually lets you know about the setting right at the beginning of a story, so that is a good place to look for information about it. *Where* does the story take place? Does it take place in our country or in a country far away? Does it take place at the beach, in a city, on a farm, or somewhere else? Does it take place inside or outside? The setting of a story also includes when it takes place, so be sure to notice that, too: Is the story happening right now? Long ago? Sometime in the future? In lots of stories, the setting changes a bit during the story. Try to decide where and when the story *mostly* takes place. Make sure you can find details about the setting.

<u>Strategy for writing</u>
1. Tell <u>where</u> and <u>when</u> the story takes place (its setting).
2. Tell one detail about this setting.
3. Tell another detail about this setting.

This story takes place _____

_____.

One detail about this setting is _____

_____.

Another detail about this setting is _____

_____.

> **A3-a: Briefly summarize this story. (fiction)**
> **A3-b: Summarize the main things that happened in this [book].**
> **(fiction, nonfiction)**

Grade level: 2-3

Teaching tips: Teachers tell me continually that this is one of the most difficult objectives for their students to master. There are several reasons for why summarizing is such a challenge. First, in the early primary grades, we ask students to do something that is similar to but not exactly like summarizing: retelling. Retelling requires that students give a blow-by-blow account of a text; no detail should be left out. (I question whether this is an authentic reader response. Nonetheless, it is the way comprehension is evaluated on numerous early-reading assessments.)

Just when kids are getting good at retelling, we tell them we don't want all those small details anymore. We want the abbreviated, abridged version, only the highlights! That is summarizing! Helping children move from including *everything* to including the bare essentials is an uphill battle. Young children are not good at sorting essentials from non-essentials. Perfecting the art of summarizing takes lots of practice.

The mastery of this objective is further complicated when teachers ask students to summarize stories that can't actually be summarized—at least according to the criteria we have established. Teachers typically tell students that a good summary includes *all* story elements. Then we ask students to "summarize chapter three." This most likely will not work because all story elements will not be present in any given chapter of most chapter books. Similarly, many picture books that we *think* are "stories" do not follow a traditional story grammar.

Again, our old favorite, *Alexander and the Terrible, Horrible, No Good, Very Bad Day* by Judith Viorst, does not have a traditional "story" structure. Alexander encounters one problem after the next—and none of these problems are ever resolved. Eventually the day simply ends. Another example, *Can I Bring My Pterodactyl to School, Ms. Johnson?* by Lois Grambling, is a great example of fluency in the invention of multiple ideas. But there is no central problem and no solution. I frequently seat myself in the picture-book section of school libraries, looking for texts for students to summarize. Invariably, the stack of picture books that *won't* work for summarizing all of the story elements is considerably taller than those that *will* work.

For stories that are basically lists of events (like the *Alexander* and *Pterodactyl* stories mentioned before), ask students to simply "summarize the events in the story." (Just list the main events in order.) This is actually easier than writing a story summary and is a good way for your children to begin the task of summarizing.

Texts for teaching about summarizing

Primary
- *A Chair for My Mother* by Vera B. Williams+
- *Amazing Grace* by Mary Hoffman and Shay Youngblood +
- *Big Al* by Andrew Clements
- *Can I Bring My Pterodactyl to School, Ms. Johnson?* by Lois Grambling
- *Chrysanthemum* by Kevin Henkes
- *Dandelion* by Don Freeman
- *Frederick* by Leo Lionni
- *Kitten's First Full Moon* by Kevin Henkes
- *Koala Lou* by Mem Fox
- *Stellaluna* by Janell Cannon
- *Tacky the Penguin* by Helen Lester
- *The Gigantic Turnip* by Aleksei Tolstoy
- *The Honest-to-Goodness Truth* by Patricia C. McKissack+
- *The Princess and the Pizza* by Mary Jane Auch
- *Too Many Tamales* by Gary Soto+

Intermediate
- *A Bad Case of Stripes* by David Shannon
- *Aunt Chip and the Great Triple Creek Dam Affair* by Patricia Polacco
- *Clever Beatrice* by Margaret Willey
- *Down the Road* by Alice Schertle+
- *Melissa Parkington's Beautiful, Beautiful Hair* by Pat Brisson
- *Rotten Richie and the Ultimate Dare* by Patricia Polacco
- *Sadako* by Eleanor Coerr
- *The Name Jar* by Yangsook Choi+
- *The Paperbag Princess* by Robert N. Munsch
- *Thunder Cake* by Patricia Polacco
- *When Marian Sang* by Pam Munoz Ryan+

Name: _____ **Date:** _____

A3-a: Briefly summarize this story.

<u>Strategy for reading</u>
Think about all of the different parts of a story: characters, setting, problem, events, solution, ending. At the beginning of a story, look for places where the author is telling you about the characters, the setting, and the problem. In the middle of the story, look for events or places where characters are trying to solve the problem. (Look for *important* events.) At the end of the story, look for the solution to the problem and notice how the story ends.

<u>Strategy for writing</u>
1. Tell the main character, setting, and problem.
2. Tell 2 or 3 things that happen before the problem gets solved.
3. Tell how the problem gets solved and what happens at the end.

The main character in this story is _____.

The story takes place _____.

The problem that gets the story going is _____
_____.

Something that happens before the problem gets solved is _____
_____.

Something else that happens before the problem gets solved is ____
_____.

The problem gets solved by _____
_____.

Here is how the story ends: _____
_____.

Name: _____ **Date:** _____

A3-b: Summarize the main things that happened in this [book].

Strategy for reading
Think about the different things that happen in this [story]. What happens first?
What happens next? Does something else happen? What happens at the very
end? Try to keep track of the important things that happen. Try to remember
them in order.

Strategy for writing
1. Tell what happens *first.*
2. Tell what happens *next.*
3. Tell what happens *after that.*
4. Tell what happens *at the end.*

The first thing that happens is _____
_____ .
The next thing that happens is _____
_____ .
After that _____
_____ .
At the end _____
_____ .

A3-c: Briefly summarize this article/informational text. (nonfiction)

Grade level: 2-3

Teaching tips: Making the distinction between the information needed for a summary of *narrative text* and a summary of *non-narrative (expository)* text is challenging for even our very capable students. From the earliest days of kindergarten, we labor over those parts needed to summarize a story and ask students: "Who was the main character? What was his problem? How did the problem get solved?" Then at some point, perhaps a year or two later, we ask students to summarize a news article or informational text—for example, an event in the life of a sports hero or a current event about an earthquake or a hurricane somewhere in the world. That old, familiar story summary format just doesn't work!

For a summary of non-narrative text, kids need to tune in to the *five Ws* (and *H*): *who, what, when, where, why,* and *how. Who* is this article mainly about? *What* happened? They need to locate the answers to those other "*W/H*" questions, too.

In order to make this manageable for children, find text that is constructed to respond to these questions. News articles *should* follow this format. Passages about an event in the life of a notable person should also qualify. Letters are often written to supply information. In addition to the many news periodicals accessible to schools and written for students at varying grade levels, some local newspapers have "kids' pages" that introduce timely topics in a manner that is both instructive and entertaining—and easy to read. There are also books (some quite cute) that use a newspaper, letter, or journal format to convey their message. These resources are well suited to students just beginning to learn the skill of summarizing non-narrative text.

Texts for teaching students to summarize non-narrative (expository) text

Primary
- *Dear Mr. Blueberry* by Simon James
- *Dear Peter Rabbit* by Alma Flor Ada
- *The Jolly Postman* by Janet and Allan Ahlberg
- *With Love, Little Red Hen* by Alma Flor Ada
- *Yours Truly, Goldilocks* by Alma Flor Ada

Intermediate
- *Extra! Extra! Fairy-Tale News from Hidden Forest* by Alma Flor Ada
- *The Secret Knowledge of Grown-Ups* by David Wisniewski
- *The Secret Knowledge of Grown-Ups: The Second File* by David Wisniewski

A3-c: Briefly summarize this article/informational text.

<u>Strategy for reading</u>
Remember the five *Ws* and *H*: *who, what, when, where, why,* and *how*. A news article or other informational text is usually written to answer these questions. Often, the author provides the answers to these questions right at the *beginning* of the article, so be sure to look for this information in the first couple of paragraphs. If it is a long article, the middle and end of it probably give *details* about the five *Ws* to help you better understand the topic.

<u>Strategy for writing</u>
1. Tell *what* happened.
2. Tell *who* was involved (the most important person or people).
3. Tell *when* and *where* the event took place.
4. Tell *why* or *how* it happened (one or two reasons).

Here is *what* happened: _____
_____.
The person (or people) involved were: _____
_____.
The time and place where this happened were: _____
_____.
This happened because _____
_____.

A4-a: Predict will happen next in this story. (fiction)

Grade level: K-3

Teaching tips: Young children love to "guess what will happen next" in a story. Thus begins the art of making predictions! For the most part, even students in kindergarten do a pretty good job of this, and their predictions are generally logical—based on their knowledge of what has come before and what will *most likely* happen next. Early readers focus not only on obvious comprehension clues, but on picture clues and rhyme. The story *Is Your Mama a Llama?* is a perfect example of a story with multiple clues for making a prediction.

Using background knowledge to make a prediction is a good *thinking* strategy but, by itself, is not a good *reading* strategy. Students should always reference what they know about a topic (their schema) in order to predict appropriately. But if they do not simultaneously reference the text, their prediction does not truly reflect *reading* comprehension.

As students move through the primary grades and into the intermediate grades, their predictions should be based more solidly on the content of what they read. Stories that generate the best predictions typically have lots of adventure and action—which inspires students to keep thinking about the next thing that will probably happen. An example of this type of "action-packed" adventure would be any of the Dr. Seuss books. Or, at a slightly more advanced level, students begin to make predictions about the decisions that characters make based on their motives and what they care about. *Down the Road* by Alice Schertle is an example of a primary-level text where students' understanding of character will lead them to anticipate what the main character will probably do next.

Older students should also begin to make predictions based on what they know about favorite authors and familiar genres. *Was the story written by Patricia Polacco? What kinds of stories does Patricia Polacco write? Is the story a fairy tale? What do you expect to find in a fairy tale?* Knowledge of the topic, the author, and the genre all helps students to make logical predictions.

Texts for teaching making predictions about what might happen next in a story

Primary
- *Arthur's Birthday* by Marc Brown (or other *Arthur* books)
- *Is Your Mama a Llama?* by Deborah Guarino
- *Lunch* by Denise Fleming
- *The Day Jimmy's Boa Ate the Wash* by Trinka Hakes Noble
- *Where the Wild Things Are* by Maurice Sendak

Intermediate

- *Down the Road* by Alice Schertle+
- *Hey, Little Ant* by Phillip M. and Hannah Hoose
- *Probuditi!* by Chris Van Allsburg
- *The Polar Express*, *The Wretched Stone* and others by Chris Van Allsburg
- *White Socks Only* by Evelyn Coleman+

A4-a: Predict what will happen next in this story.

<u>Strategy for reading</u>
Think about what has happened in the story so far and how the characters *usually* act. Also think about what the characters learned from this experience. Based on this, what do you think might happen *next*?

<u>Strategy for writing</u>
1. Tell what you think will happen next.
2. Tell why you think this will probably happen. Be sure to use the word *because* and an example from the story. (Think about what has happened so far and how the characters usually act.)
3. Tell what the character learned from this experience.

I predict that the next thing that happens will be _____
_____.

I think this will probably happen because *before this* in the story:

_____
_____.

This is what the character learned: _____
_____
_____.

> **A4-b:** If the author added another paragraph to the end of the story (or article), it would **most likely** tell about _____. Use information from the story (or article) to support your answer. (fiction, nonfiction)

Grade level: 1-3

Teaching tips: Children tend to like this question—though they're not necessarily good at answering it. They enjoy pondering what might happen next if the author added another paragraph to the story (or article). Where their thinking goes off track sometimes is that they focus on the events at the beginning of the story or article. They don't focus clearly enough on the events at the end of the text: *Did the problem get solved? If so, how are the characters feeling about each other now? Will they do something together? What would they be likely to do?* Their response should take into account what occurred at the very end of the story.

Some texts intentionally leave readers "hanging." In that case, the story or article practically begs for further insights from the reader: *Given everything you have learned so far, how do you think this situation will get resolved?* Chris Van Allsburg's books leave the reader with many loose ends. Some of these texts may be too sophisticated for primary students. But older readers love the creative thinking that predictions of this sort require.

Texts for teaching about adding another paragraph to a story or article

Primary
- *Big Al* by Andrew Clements
- *Corduroy* by Don Freeman
- *Dear Mr. Blueberry* by Simon James
- *Fireflies* by Julie Brinckloe
- *Miss Rumphius* by Barbara Cooney
- *Stand Tall, Molly Lou Melon* by Patty Lovell
- *The Honest-to-Goodness Truth* by Patricia C. McKissack+
- *Too Many Tamales* by Gary Soto+

Intermediate
- *A Picnic in October* by Eve Bunting
- *Baseball Saved Us* by Ken Mochizuki
- *Freedom Summer* by Deborah Wiles+
- *Heroes* by Ken Mochizuki+
- *The Memory String* by Eve Bunting
- *The Other Side* by Jacqueline Woodson+
- *The Wretched Stone* by Chris Van Allsburg
- *Tomás and the Library Lady* by Pat Mora+

A4-b: **If the author added another paragraph to the end of the story (or article), it would <u>most likely</u> tell about _____ . Use information from the story (or article) to support your answer.**

<u>Strategy for reading</u>
In order to figure out what will probably happen next, you need to know what happened right before the end of the story (or article). Had the problem been solved? How are the characters feeling about each other now? Use that information to decide what would <u>most likely</u> happen if the author had added another paragraph to the end of the text.

<u>Strategy for writing</u>
1. Tell what would most likely happen next if the author added another paragraph.
2. Tell *why* that would probably happen next (based on what happened at the end of the story/article).

If the author had added another paragraph to this story/article, it most likely would have told about _____

_____

_____ .

This would probably happen next because _____

_____

_____ .

Developing an Interpretation

The biggest issue with this strand is that teachers do not expose students to some of the objectives as often as they should. If students are not exposed to certain questions, it is hard for them to know how to respond. For example, teachers seldom ask children why an author included a particular paragraph in a story. Even young children can identify the kind of information an author is giving them in different parts of a text—but they are not typically asked to think about a text in this way.

By asking young students to respond to the eight questions suggested here divided among three general areas, they will begin to interpret text from many different perspectives. They will become more aware of the structure and genre of a text as well as specific information included in a text that supports a conclusion.

The "B" strand: Developing an interpretation	
B1: Identify or infer the author's use of structure/ organizational patterns	**B1-a**: What caused _____ to happen in the story? (fiction) **B1-b**: What happened at the beginning, in the middle, and at the end of the story or informational text? (fiction, nonfiction) **B1-c**: Compare these two characters: _____ and ____. (fiction) **B1-d**: Can this part of the [story/text] be described as: a definition, a description, an explanation, a conversation, an opinion, an argument, or a comparison? How do you know? (fiction, nonfiction)
B2: Draw conclusions about the author's purpose for choosing a genre or for including or omitting specific details in text	**B2-a**: Why does the author include paragraph ___? (fiction, nonfiction) **B2-b**: Why did the author write a [poem/story/informational article/nonfiction book] about this? (fiction, nonfiction)
B3: Use evidence from the text to support a conclusion	**B3-a**: Prove that [character/person] is very _____. (fiction, nonfiction) **B3-b**: Which facts show that _____? (nonfiction)

B1-a: What caused _____ to happen in the story? (fiction)

Grade level: 1-3

Teaching tips: Young students would have an easier time addressing cause and effect if we began with the effect and then worked backward to have them figure out the cause. This works because the outcome is often a lot more concrete than the situation that led up to it. Young children and struggling readers are very concrete in their thinking, so beginning here makes the task more manageable for them.

Students can be asked to respond to cause and effect questions at two different points in a story: the *problem* and the situation that led to the problem, or the *solution* and the events that led to the solution. In both cases, the response would be fairly brief.

Use the cause-and-effect graphic organizer to help students visualize this type of text structure.

Texts for teaching about cause/effect

Primary
- *Big Al* by Andrew Clements
- *Julius, the Baby of the World* by Kevin Henkes
- *Miss Rumphius* by Barbara Cooney
- *My Dog is Lost* by Ezra Jack Keats
- *Rotten Richie and the Ultimate Dare* by Patricia Polacco
- *Someday a Tree* by Eve Bunting
- *Too Many Tamales* by Gary Soto+

Intermediate
- *Coming On Home Soon* by Jacqueline Woodson+
- *Freedom Summer* by Deborah Wiles+
- *Mama Loves Me from Away* by Pat Brisson
- *Nettie's Trip South* by Ann Turner+
- *Sister Anne's Hands* by Marybeth Lorbiecki+
- *Sweet Clara and the Freedom Quilt* by Deborah Hopkinson+
- *The Rough-Face Girl* by Rafe Martin+

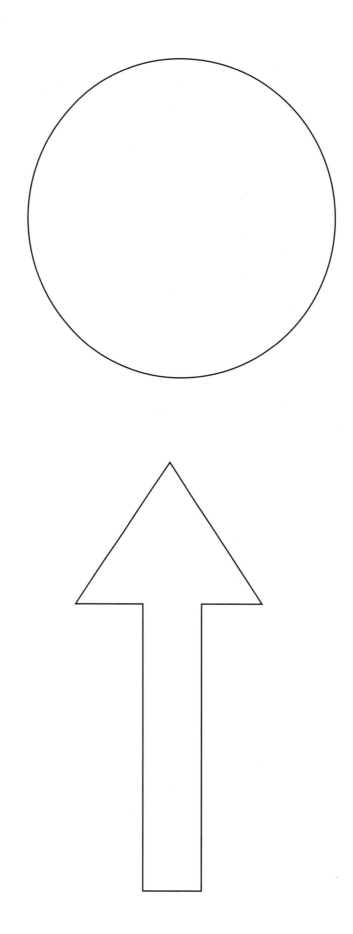

CAUSE AND EFFECT

Name: _____ **Date:** _____

B1-a: What caused _____ to happen in the story?

Strategy for reading
Think about the problem in the story? What caused that problem to happen?
OR: Think about what happened in the end. What helped to solve the problem?

Strategy for writing
    1. Tell what the problem was.
    2. Tell what caused that problem to happen.
OR
    1. Tell what happened in the end.
    2. Tell what helped to solve the problem.

The problem was _____

_____.

The problem was caused by: _____

_____.

In the end here is what happened: _____

_____.

The problem got solved because _____

_____.

B1-b: What happened at the beginning, in the middle, and at the end of the story or informational text? (fiction, nonfiction)

Grade level: K-3

Teaching tips: This is an objective that is appropriate for even very young children and encourages them to understand the sequence of a story or information explained in a text. Before addressing the actual objective, introduce the words *beginning, middle*, and *end*. Have children practice opening a book to the *beginning,* to the *middle*, and to the *end*.

Stories with lots of action are useful for teaching this objective. In these types of books, there is a well-defined problem that gets the story going at the beginning, followed by a variety of events in the middle, and then at the end, a solution. Teach lessons on *beginning, middle,* and *end* before addressing summarizing, or even retelling.

Informational "chain of events" books are also well matched to this objective and can be useful for a nonfiction focus. When using this type of text, you may wish to have students include more "middle" events in their response depending on the number of steps or events in the "chain."

Use the sequence-of-events graphic organizer to help students visualize *beginning, middle*, and *end*.

Texts for teaching about beginning, middle, and end

Primary
Stories with a clear beginning, middle, and end
- *Kitten's First Full Moon* by Kevin Henkes
- *Officer Buckle and Gloria* by Peggy Rathmann
- *Miss Bridie Chose a Shovel* by Leslie Connor
- *The Story of Jumping Mouse* by John Steptoe
- *Thunder Cake* by Patricia Polacco

"Chain of Events" books
- *Apple Pie Tree* by Zoe Hall
- *Charlie Needs a Cloak* by Tomie dePaola
- *From Caterpillar to Butterfly* by Deborah Heiligman
- *From Seed to Plant* by Gail Gibbons
- *From Tadpole to Frog* by Wendy Pfeffer

Intermediate

Stories with a clear beginning, middle, and end

- *A Bad Case of Stripes* by David Shannon
- *Down the Road* by Alice Schertle+
- *Gettin' Through Thursday* by Melrose Cooper+
- *Melissa Parkington's Beautiful, Beautiful Hair* by Pat Brisson
- *Salt in His Shoes: Michael Jordan in Pursuit of a Dream* by Deloris and Roslyn M. Jordan+
- *Tea with Milk* by Allen Say+
- *The Name Jar* by Yangsook Choi+

"Chain of Events" books or books with a clear sequence

- *Follow the Drinking Gourd* by Jeanette Winter+
- *How is a Crayon Made?* By Oz Charles
- *One Tiny Turtle: Read and Wonder* by Nicola Davies
- *The Emperor Lays an Egg* by Brenda Z. Guiberson
- *The Life Cycle of a Butterfly*, *The Life Cycle of a Flower* and other *Life Cycle* books by Bobbie Kalman

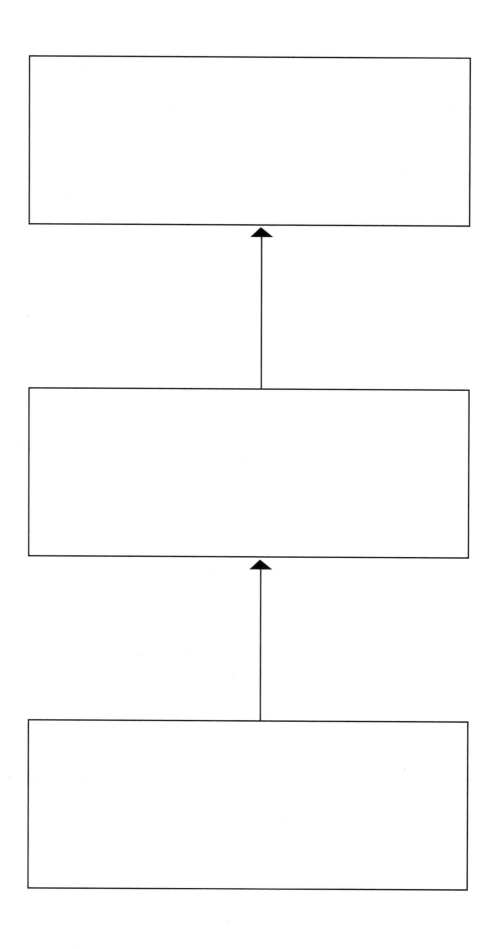

SEQUENCE OF EVENTS

B1-b: What happened at the beginning, in the middle, and at the end of the story or informational text?

<u>Strategy for reading</u>
Look for something important that happens at the *beginning* of the text (in the first few pages). Now find something that happens in the *middle*. (There should be lots of pages *before* the middle and *after* the middle.) Now find something that happens at the *end* (in the last few pages).

<u>Strategy for writing</u>
1. Write something important that happens at the *beginning* of the story or informational book.
2. Write something important that happens in the *middle* of the story or informational book.
3. Write something important that happens at the *end* of the story or informational book.

At the *beginning* _____
_____ .
In the *middle* _____
_____ .
At the *end* _____
_____ .

B1-c: Compare these two characters: _____ and _____. (fiction)

Grade level: K-3

Teaching tips: I've seen children as young as kindergarten and first grade compare characters with relative ease. They even know how to use a Venn diagram to represent the similarities and differences among characters! The important thing with this objective is to help students identify *significant* similarities and differences. "One character is a girl and the other is a boy," may not account for the important attributes that separate one character from another.

Meeting this objective becomes more complicated when the central character is compared to the "societal norm" rather to another specific character (or person). An example of this at the primary level might be *Tacky the Penguin* by Helen Lester. In this story, Tacky's creativity is compared to the attitudes of his more "proper" penguin friends. At the intermediate level, the same theme, daring to be different, is celebrated in the book *What's the Matter with Albert* by Freida Wishinsky. Note the contrast, as well in *Ruby Bridges* (Robert Coles) where Ruby's family has a very different view of desegregation than other folks in her New Orleans school.

Select texts for teaching this objective where there is a stark contrast between the main character and another character (or everyone else). Comparing "real people" in nonfiction text is also a good way to teach this objective.

Using a Venn diagram to help visualize similarities and differences among characters is a good way for children to organize their thinking before writing a narrative response. If there are no important similarities between the characters, a T-chart might be more useful than a Venn diagram.

Texts for teaching about comparing characters/people

Primary
- *A Picture Book of Jackie Robinson* by David A. Adler+
- *Frederick* by Leo Lionni
- *Stand Tall, Molly Lou Melon* by Patty Lovell
- *Tacky the Penguin* by Helen Lester
- *The Lion Who Wanted to Love* by Giles Andreae and David Wojtowycz
- *The Pain and the Great One* by Judy Blume
- *This is the Dream* by Diane Z. Shore and Jessica Alexander

Intermediate

- *Meet Danitra Brown* by Nikki Grimes
- *Teammates* by Peter Golenbock+
- *The Other Side* by Jacqueline Woodson+
- *The Paperbag Princess* by Robert N. Munsch
- *The Story of Ruby Bridges* by Robert Coles+
- *Weslandia* by Paul Fleischman
- *What's the Matter with Albert: The Story of Albert Einstein* by Frieda Wishinsky
- *Wings* by Christopher Myers

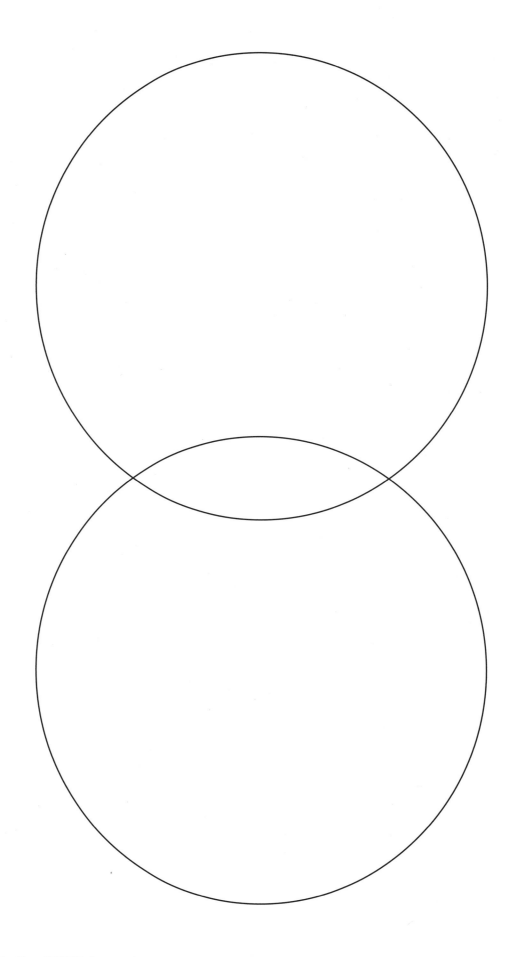

COMPARE AND CONTRAST

COMPARING DIFFERENCES BETWEEN CHARACTERS

Character 1:	Character 2 (or everyone else):

B1-c: Compare these (two) characters: _____ and _____ .

Strategy for reading
Pay close attention to the details about the main character as you read. What makes this person special or different from another character—or lots of other people? (It might be something they did, something that happened to them, or something that was important to them.)

Strategy for writing
1. Tell something special about the main character that makes him/her *different* from the other character(s).
2. Give an example that *shows* what was important to the main character.
3. Now tell something special about the second character (or other people) that shows what is important to them.
4. Give an example that *shows* what you mean.

Something that was important to _____ was_____
Character 1

_____ .

This character shows this by _____

_____ .

This was different from the way _____
Character 2 (or other characters)

felt about _____ .

An example that shows this is _____

_____ .

Grade level: 2-3

Teaching tips: This is the kind of objective that is quite easy for students to master if their teacher has taught it—and almost impossible if the objective has not been taught. It's all about the academic language: *definition, description, explanation, conversation, opinion, argument, comparison.*

I suggest that teachers display brief kid-friendly definitions of each term somewhere in the classroom where students can easily refer to them—and then reference the terms often while reading aloud to students or when the students are reading texts during small-group instruction: "Oh, look, the author is making a *comparison* here." Or, "Notice how the author is giving a great *description* of the setting in this paragraph."

The following definitions of terms I have provided may be just right for your class, or you may need to modify them to make them more basic. Either way, it is probably better to write each one separately on a sentence strip and hang the strips up individually, rather than creating a single chart with all of the words and definitions listed. That way, each term will really stand out!

Texts appropriate for both primary and intermediate levels for teaching about literary terms such as *definition, description, explanation, conversation, opinion, argument,* and *comparison*

Definition
Alphabet or concept books that provide brief descriptions of each entry, such as alphabet books by Jerry Palotta

Description
Some authors use lots of description as they write, providing wonderful visual images: Jane Yolen, Cynthia Rylant, Charlotte Zolatow, Libba Moore Gray, Thomas Locker, Faith Ringgold, Nikki Grimes, and Patricia MacLachlan.

Primary
- *All the Places to Love by Patricia MacLachlan*
- *One Tiny Turtle: Read and Wonder by Nicola Davies*
- *Welcome to the Green House and Welcome to the Sea of Sand by Jane Yolen*
- *When Sophie Gets Angry—Really, Really Angry by Molly Bang*
- *Young Cornrows Callin Out the Moon by Ruth Forman+*

Intermediate

- *Hoops* and *Home Run* by Robert Burleigh+
- *In November and Scarecrow* by Cynthia Rylant
- *Is that You, Winter?* by Stephen Gammell
- *Owen and Mzee: The True Story of a Remarkable Friendship* by Isabella Hatkoff, Craig Hatkoff, and Dr. Paula Kahumbu
- *Tulip Sees America* by Cynthia Rylant
- *Water Dance, Cloud Dance, Mountain Dance,* and other books by Thomas Locker

Explanation

"How-to" and "All-about" books

- *Firefighters* by Christopher Mitten
- *From Seed to Plant* by Gail Gibbons
- *How a House is Built* by Gail Gibbons
- *How is a Crayon Made?* by Oz Charles
- *What is a Scientist?* by Barbara Lehn

Conversation

Plays (There are numerous resources available for reader's theater)
Any story with dialogue (too numerous to list)

Opinion

Letters to the editor
Books told from more than one point of view

- *Dear Mother, Dear Daughter* by Jane Yolen and Heidi Stemple
- *Hey, Little Ant* by Phillip M. and Hannah Hoose
- *Talkin' About Bessie: The Story of Aviator Elizabeth Coleman* by Nikki Grimes+
- *The Pain and the Great One* by Judy Blume

Argument

Books about characters who fight to change laws or people who stand up for what they believe. Some possibilities would be stories about characters who participated in the Underground Railroad or Civil Rights movement.

- *Dinner at Aunt Connie's House* by Faith Ringgold+
- *Minty: A Story of Young Harriet Tubman* by Alan Schroeder+
- *My Dream of Martin Luther King* by Faith Ringgold+
- *Nobody Owns the Sky: The Story of Bessie Coleman* by Reeve Lindbergh+
- *Sweet Clara and the Freedom Quilt* by Deborah Hopkinson+
- *When Marian Sang* by Pam Munoz Ryan+

Comparison

Any of the books listed previously for "Compare/Contrast" (B1-c)

DEFINING THE PURPOSE OF A SECTION OF TEXT

Definition: An important word (term) is explained in language that makes it easier to understand.

Comparison: The similarities and differences between two or more things are explained.

Description: The author helps you picture something by using adjectives or giving you lots of details about it.

Opinion: The author explains what he thinks or feels about something. Someone else might feel differently. An opinion can not be *proven* to be true because it is not a *fact*.

Conversation: Two or more people are talking together. You might see quotation marks.

Explanation: The author gives you information about something, such as how it works or how it is made.

Argument: Someone is trying hard to convince (or persuade) another character that his or her point of view is right.

Name: _____ **Date:** _____

B1-d: **Can this part of the [story/text] be described as: a definition, a description, an explanation, a conversation, an opinion, an argument, or a comparison? How do you know?**

Strategy for reading

Authors give you information in lots of different ways. Sometimes they *describe* things. Sometimes they tell you their *opinion* about something. Sometimes they give you information in a *conversation* that two or more characters are having together. They give you information in other ways, too. As you read, notice what the author is doing to give you information.

Strategy for writing
1. Tell what the author is doing in a particular part of a text to give you information. (Is this part of the text a definition, a description, an explanation, a conversation, an opinion, an argument, or a comparison?)
2. Explain how you know that this is a definition, a description, an explanation, a conversation, an opinion, an argument, or a comparison.

This part of the text is a _____ .

I know this is a _____ because_____

_____

_____ .

B2-a: Why does the author include paragraph _____?
(fiction, nonfiction)

Grade level: 2-3

Teaching tips: This is an objective that is often omitted or under-represented in teachers' day-to-day literacy instruction. How often do you ask your students, "What kind of information is the author giving us in this paragraph (or this part of the text)? What does the author want us to understand here?" If we just asked these questions more often, students would be better able to meet this objective because once they are used to looking at text in this way, it is not hard to interpret the reason for including an identified portion of text.

The big question students must be able to answer is: "What do we know now that we would not have known if the author hadn't included this paragraph (or portion of the text)?" This is different from the preceding objectives because in this case we do not just need to know that the author is giving us a *description*. We need to identify precisely *what* the author is describing and *why* the author is describing it.

To teach this objective, look for a paragraph or portion of a text where the author is giving the reader specific information about a character, setting, problem, event, or solution to a story, or a fact about some nonfiction topic. Have students read this portion of text, and then cover it up with their hand. Ask, "What would we *not* have known about [Grandma] if the author hadn't included this paragraph? What is the author trying to show us about [Grandma]?"

By physically covering up the evidence, even young children can figure out that an author included a particular paragraph because she wanted us to know that Grandma was a person who showed her love by making chocolate chip cookies for her grandchildren or that she might have been "getting on in years," but she was still as feisty and as determined as ever.

Any text can be used to teach this objective. Look especially for recurring details where the author gives multiple examples that demonstrate a particular trait, feeling, or motive. Such recurring details make later events in the text predictable, almost inevitable. For example, in the story *Minty* by Alan Schroeder, a fictionalized biography about the childhood of Harriet Tubman, the author includes many passages that demonstrate the stubbornness and persistence of Harriet along with the cruelty with which she was treated. By including several details that show these same traits, it becomes quite predictable that Harriet will ultimately run away, in order to escape slavery.

Texts with recurring details for teaching about why an author included a particular paragraph or portion of a text

Primary

- *Alexander and the Terrible, Horrible, No Good, Very Bad Day* by Judith Viorst
- *Big Al* by Andrew Clements
- *Mia Hamm: Winners Never Quit* by Mia Hamm
- *Mr. George Baker* by Amy Hest+
- *Nobody Owns the Sky: The Story of Bessie Coleman* by Reeve Lindbergh+
- *Peppe the Lamplighter* by Elisa Bartone
- *The Hello, Goodbye Window* by Norton Juster
- *The Memory Coat* by Elvira Woodruff

Intermediate

- *Almost to Freedom* by Vaunda Micheaux Nelson
- *A Picnic in October* by Eve Bunting
- *Goin' Someplace Special* by Patricia C. McKissack+
- *Hewitt Anderson's Great Big Life* by Jerdine Nolen
- *Me, All Alone at the End of the World* by M.T. Anderson
- *Minty: A Story of Young Harriet Tubman* by Alan Schroeder+
- *More than Anything Else* by Marie Bradby+
- *Remember: The Journey to School Integration* by Toni Morrison+
- *Snowflake Bentley* by Jacqueline Briggs Martin
- *Something Beautiful* by Sharon Dennis Wyeth+
- *Talkin' About Bessie: The Story of Aviator Elizabeth Coleman* by Nikki Grimes+
- *Tea with Milk* by Allen Say+
- *Tomás and the Library Lady* by Pat Mora+

B2-a: Why does the author include paragraph ___? (What did the author want you to understand?)

<u>Strategy for reading</u>
Go back and re-read this paragraph or part of the text. What is it about? Now cover it up. What would you *not* know about if that covered paragraph were not there? The author included this paragraph because he or she wanted you to understand something beyond just the words in the text. What did the author want you to understand? It might be something about a character/person, a problem, a setting, or a particular event.

<u>Strategy for writing</u>
1. Tell what this paragraph or passage is about.
2. Give one or two examples that *show* what you mean.
3. Explain what the author wanted you to understand by writing this paragraph.

This paragraph or passage is about_____ _____. Here is an example that shows what I mean: _____ _____. By including this paragraph or passage, I think the author wanted me to understand that _____ _____.

B2-b: Why did the author write a [poem/story/information article/ nonfiction book] about this topic? (fiction, nonfiction)

Grade level: 3

Teaching tips: This is another objective that classroom teachers typically spend little time addressing. We seldom consider with students, especially young students, the elements of a particular genre and why an author might have chosen that genre to share her message. But we should. Knowing the special features of a genre enhances comprehension because now readers know what to expect from the text and look for those features as they read: *Is it a fable? As a reader you are on the lookout for animals who behave like people, and a moral or lesson at the end. Is it a poem?* There will probably be some good visual images and rhyming words that will add to the sense of fluency.

Some genres may be too sophisticated for students in the primary grades or older students still struggling with literacy basics. However, there are plenty of genres that *are* within their grasp, and of course you can continue to add to the list when students are ready to move forward.

Some simple genres with which to begin might be stories, informational articles, poetry, and letters. In each case, it is important to clarify the elements of the genre in order to decide why the author selected that particular format. Consider posting these elements on sentence strips around the classroom. Follow up by asking students to tell you what to expect as they read different kinds of texts. For this objective, there is no list of texts since the list would be infinite. However, the list of genre characteristics on the following page will give you a place to begin. Add to it with ideas your students suggest. Remember, there is no "right" or "wrong" answer to a question about the choice of genre. But students must say *something*, and what they say needs to demonstrate an understanding of a genre's special features.

GENRE ELEMENTS

For getting started

- **Story:** Contains characters, a problem, a setting, events, a solution, and an ending; stories are more interesting than informational articles to most readers and are more likely to be remembered

- **Informational article:** Presents factual information in a straightforward way; uses subheadings to guide the reading; uses photos and graphics to contribute to understanding; communicate important information in a limited space (like a newspaper article)

- **Poetry:** Conveys a message in a brief format; creates a picture in your mind through imagery; uses rhyme to add to fluency

- **Letter:** Contains a greeting, closing, and, in the middle, personal information; provides the opportunity for a clear and distinctive voice since it is written to a very specific audience; the tone can be formal or informal depending on the purpose of the letter.

For more advanced readers

- **Personal narrative/memoir:** Tells about important events or people in a person's life; does not always involve a problem and a solution; written with strong feeling; describes just a portion of a person's life, not the entire life

- **Realistic fiction:** Tells a story that readers can relate to because it is believable, with characters that behave like real people and problems that could be real problems; contains all story elements

- **Historical fiction:** The purpose is to both explain and inform; may include some people and events that are real and some that are fictional; events are presented in story form

- **Biography:** Shows a person's life (usually) from birth to death with a focus on reasons for the person's success; contains typical story elements but does not necessarily contain a problem and a solution

B2-b: Why did the author write a [poem/story/ informational article/ nonfiction book] about this topic?

Strategy for reading

Think about what you know about this genre. As you are reading, look for these features. (You might be looking for story elements such as characters and setting or something else.) Think abut why the author might have wanted to use this genre to communicate his or her message: How did this genre help the author to make the message meaningful?

Strategy for writing

1. Write a topic sentence that states the genre.
2. Write one or more sentences telling why you think the author thought this would be a good genre to use to communicate his or her message. (Be sure to talk about specific features that are usually present in this genre.)
3. Give one or two examples showing that these genre features are present in this text.

The genre of this text is _____. In this genre you usually find _____

_____.

One example that shows this in this text is: _____

_____.

Another example that shows this is: _____

_____.

B3-a: Prove that [character/person] is very _____.
(fiction, nonfiction)

Grade level: K-3

Teaching tips: On the surface, this looks like an easy objective. Lots of books for primary students contain clearly drawn (almost one-dimensional) characters, and there's not much guess work involved in deciding the dominant character trait. The character is *so* kind or *so* brave that there's no mistaking the evidence that points to this trait.

If the identified trait is *kind* or *brave*, answering the question is pretty easy. But what if the trait is *considerate* or *courageous*? Now what's the problem? There are two potential problems here: Maybe students can't decode the trait word, so they have no idea what question they're actually answering. Or maybe they can decode it but do not know what the word means.

So what is a teacher to do? Certainly it is important to always work on phonics and word-identification skills as well as comprehension objectives. That will solve the first problem. To address the second problem (word meaning), teachers need to get serious about vocabulary instruction.

While there are many ways to approach the teaching of vocabulary, I think what would be most useful in this case would be to create a word wall of character trait words and add to it each time you finish a book: For example, what word would you use to describe Little Red Riding Hood? Students might say that Little Red Riding Hood is "helpful" or "friendly" or (everyone's favorite) "nice." The teacher could suggest a few additional words to extend their vocabulary and make it more specific: disobedient, foolish, careless. By continually adding to students' repertoire of character trait words, they will develop a better command of the academic vocabulary needed to respond to questions of this sort. A list of character trait words suitable for young learners is provided after the following bibliography to get you started.

Texts in which characters exhibit strong traits

Primary
- *Big Al* by Andrew Clements
- *Mia Hamm: Winners Never Quit* by Mia Hamm
- *Miss Bridie Chose a Shovel* by Leslie Connor
- *Nobody Owns the Sky: The Story of Bessie Coleman* by Reeve Lindbergh+
- *Princess Penelope's Parrot* by Helen Lester

- *Salt in His Shoes: Michael Jordan in Pursuit of a Dream* by Deloris and Roslyn M. Jordan+
- *Stand Tall, Molly Lou Melon* by Patty Lovell
- *Tacky the Penguin* by Helen Lester
- *Wemberly Worried* by Kevin Henkes

Intermediate
- *A Bad Case of Stripes* by David Shannon
- *Brothers in Hope: The Story of the Lost Boys of Sudan* by Mary Williams
- *Coming On Home Soon* by Jacqueline Woodson+
- *Floridius Bloom and the Planet of Gloom* by Lorijo Metz
- *Melissa Parkington's Beautiful, Beautiful Hair* by Pat Brisson
- *More than Anything Else* by Marie Bradby
- *Tea with Milk* by Allen Say
- *The Rough-Face Girl* by Rafe Martin
- *The Story of Ruby Bridges* by Robert Coles

CHARACTER TRAIT WORDS

Primary	Intermediate	
Brave	Confident	Innocent
Calm	Considerate	Predictable
Careful	Creative	Self-assured
Careless	Dishonest	Spiteful
Cheerful	Intelligent	Tolerant
Clever	Impatient	Trustworthy
Cross	Reliable	Assertive
Cruel	Ungrateful	Haughty
Curious	Cautious	Indifferent
Foolish	Cowardly	Meek
Fun	Dependable	Menacing
Funny	Fearless	Noble
Gloomy	Ferocious	Surly
Grumpy	Gullible	Glum
Honest	Humble	Ingenious
Kind	Loyal	Conceited
Mischievous	Optimistic	Rambunctious
Miserable	Pessimistic	Sullen
Patient	Argumentative	
Reckless	Bold	
Selfish	Envious	
Thoughtful	Faithful	
Wicked	Independent	
Wise	Insensitive	
	Irritable	
	Modest	
	Sensible	
	Stern	
	Sympathetic	
	Supportive	
	Timid	
	Unpredictable	
	Unreliable	
	Appreciative	
	Carefree	
	Demanding	

Name: _____ **Date:** _____

B3-a: Prove that [character/person] is very _____.

Strategy for reading
Think about what the describing word really means. As you are reading, find two places where the character shows this trait by the way he or she acts, talks, or thinks.

Strategy for writing
1. Write a topic sentence that includes the trait word. (Ex: Jim was very *brave*.)
2. Give one example that shows the character had this trait.
3. Give another example that shows the character had this trait.

In this story, _____ was very _____.

One example that shows this is: _____

_____

_____.

Another example that shows this is : _____

_____

_____.

B3-b: Which facts show that _____? (nonfiction)

Grade level: 1-3

Teaching tips: This objective is very similar to the preceding one, except that instead of justifying a character trait with details from a story, students now need to validate a main idea statement or conclusion based on facts in a nonfiction selection. The tricky part here is that readers need to go back to the text to find their evidence; they may not rely on their background knowledge or their imagination—as many children would like to do.

In order to prove that loggerhead turtles are really heavy, James wrote "Adult loggerheads weigh 1,000 pounds." At first I just accepted this "fact." But the more I thought about it, that seemed awfully large, even for a loggerhead. On closer examination of the text, the exact weight of a loggerhead was nowhere to be found (and was inaccurate when I later consulted another article about loggerheads). James had more or less made up his own "fact" based on the illustrations in the book and what seemed reasonable to him. Nice try, James.

To build this skill, provide students with nonfiction text they can mark up, and have them underline their evidence right in the selection. They should be able to show you the exact sentence in the text where they obtained their evidence to support a main idea. *What is...* and *What Makes...* books are perfect for primary because the information they present is basic and clear. Books in the *If You...* series are good for intermediate-grade students because the main idea is stated as a question, followed by a page of supporting evidence.

Texts for teaching young children to support a main idea with facts

Primary
- *The Emperor Lays an Egg* by Brenda Z. Guiberson
- *What is a Scientist?* by Barbara Lehn
- *What is Matter?* by Don L. Curry
- *What Makes a Magnet?* by Franklyn M. Branley

Intermediate
- *If You Lived in Colonial Times* by Ann McGovern
- *If You Traveled on the Underground Railroad* by Ellen Levine (and many other titles, all published by Scholastic)
- *Immigrant Kids* by Russell Freedman
- *Journey to Ellis Island* by Carol Bierman
- *Lincoln: A Photobiography, The Wright Brothers,* and others by Russell Freedman

Name: _____ **Date:** _____

B3-b: Which facts show that _____?

Strategy for reading
This question goes mostly with nonfiction reading. Think about what you are
being asked to prove by looking carefully at the question. As you read, find
two places where the author is giving information about this. Then try to find
two facts that really prove that what you are saying is true. Think about which
information is the best support.

Strategy for writing
1. Write a topic sentence that restates (from the question) what you need to
   prove.
2. Give one fact that proves this.
3. Give another fact that proves this.

I can prove from my reading that _____
_____.

One fact that proves this is: _____

_____

_____.

Another fact that proves this is: _____

_____

_____.

It's a sign of the times that *making connections* gets its very own strand! The notion of *connecting to text* is looming large on the literacy horizon these days as research points to the power of personal connections in improving students' comprehension. Many teachers incorporate the explicit teaching of the *connecting* strategy into their daily literacy instruction. Core programs make sure that *connections* are well represented before, during, and after reading. State assessments tap into the *connections* phenomenon as well, requiring students to demonstrate their skill in responding to open-ended questions about personal connections to text.

So with all of the time and attention devoted to *making connections*, why aren't some students doing better in this area on literacy assessments? I have a few hypotheses. First, students sometimes write elaborate, long-winded accounts of their own experiences related to a problem or event in a text, so long-winded in fact that they completely forget to return to the text to make the actual connection. This, of course, spells doom when it comes to scoring their response.

A second issue that undermines the quality of students' responses to connection questions is their lack of expertise in responding to open-ended questions in general. Making text-to-self connections will always appear in the form of an open-ended question because the multiple-choice format just won't work for a personal connection. If students do not understand how to produce a written response that is organized, includes relevant details, and is fluent enough to be easily read, they will receive little credit for their answer—even if it is basically accurate.

A third concern is that students make superficial connections or claim they have no connection at all. The text says, "A dog named Shep saved his entire family from their burning house by breaking through a screen and racing to the house next door to alert the neighbor. Later, the entire community cheered when Shep received a medal for his bravery."

One student connected: "My cousin has a dog named Shep." A connection without more substance than this will not impress a scorer.

Another student responded, "I don't have any connection to this. My dog never saved anyone from a burning house." Too many students think that the only valid personal connection is one that parallels an exact event in a text.

All three of these reasons could account for students' poor performance as they respond to text in a personal way. Still, I think there is another, more significant reason. Re-read the title of this chapter. Is it *only* about connecting? Somehow, the other form of personal response, *reacting to text*, gets lost in our zeal to help children make connections.

Reacting to text requires students to think about their reading in ways that are different from making connections: *What surprised you as you read this story? What did you find interesting?* And perhaps most basic of all: *Did you like this book?*

The irony of this is that when you think about it, aren't we teaching children to read so they will have a personal reaction to their reading? We get so focused on having them find the main idea or identifying character traits, or sequencing events that we forget to ask: *So, did you like the book?*

By asking the eight questions that follow, we will be offering readers a range of possibilities, both connections and reactions, for personal responses. The following questions are suitable for young students or students at higher grade levels still struggling with literature response:

The "C" strand: Making reader/text connections	
C1: Connect the text to personal experience, another text, or the outside world	**C1-a**: Think about someone who was [helpful]. Tell how that experience was like the experience of _____ in the story. (fiction) **C1-b**: Make a personal connection. Show how something that happened in the story is like something that happened in your own life. (fiction) **C1-c**: Which character in the story would you like to know and why? (fiction) **C1-d**: Using information in the story, explain whether you would ever want to _____. (fiction)
C2: Make a personal response to the text	**C2-a**: Which part of the [story/article] do you think was *most* important? Use information from the [story/article] to explain why you chose that part. (fiction, nonfiction) **C2-b**: Which part of this [story/article] was most interesting or surprising to you? Why? (fiction, nonfiction) **C2-c**: Did you like this [story/article]? Why or why not? (fiction, nonfiction) **C2-d**: What was your first reaction to this text? Explain. (fiction, nonfiction)

> **C1-a: Think about someone who was [helpful]. Tell how that experience was like the experience of _____ in the story. (fiction)**

Grade level: K-3

Teaching tips: When the objective identifies the kind of connection that needs to be made, even the youngest learners can meet the challenge. As you teach this objective, help students understand that the connection to their life does not need to mimic the exact experience of the character in the text. For example, using the attribute in the question above, if the character in the story was *helpful* by helping his mom wash the dishes, your personal connection does not have to have anything to do with helping wash the dishes. Your personal connection could be about helping to take care of your little brother or helping your teacher pass out papers. Explain this broader view of connections to students, and model for them responses that go beyond text-specific experiences.

To avoid the problem of writing at length about a personal experience and neglecting to return to the text to make the actual connection, encourage students to *begin* (rather than end) with the evidence from the text: "In the story, Joshua helped his mom by cleaning up the dishes every night after supper. That is like my life because I help my mom by taking care of my little brother when she is making dinner…" More elaboration can be added to strengthen the response. But even without these extra details, all necessary components of the question have been addressed.

The best sources for teaching text-to-self connections are realistic stories or personal narratives. Students easily relate to texts about characters of a similar age who live in a place similar to where they live: They connect to "real" kids involved in problems with family, friends, school, etc.—just like problems they might experience.

Texts for teaching about connections to self

Primary

- ✓ *Alexander and the Terrible, Horrible, No Good, Very Bad Day* by Judith Viorst
- *Annabelle Swift, Kindergartner* by Amy Schwartz
- *Bigmama's* by Donald Crews+
- ✓ *Corduroy* by Don Freeman
- ✓ *Ira Sleeps Over* by Bernard Waber
- *Now One Foot, Now the Other* by Tomie dePaola
- *Pigsty* by Mark Teague
- *Tell Me a Story Mama* by Angela Johnson+
- *The Pain and the Great One* by Judy Blume
- *The Relatives Came* by Cynthia Rylant

Intermediate

- *Brothers in Hope: The Story of the Lost Boys of Sudan* by Mary Williams+
- *Calling the Doves* by Juan Felipe Herrera
- *Dream: A Tale of Wonder, Wisdom & Wishes* by Susan V. Bosak
- *In My Momma's Kitchen* by Jerdine Nolen
- *Melissa Parkington's Beautiful, Beautiful Hair* by Pat Brisson
- *Odd Boy Out: Young Albert Einstein* by Don Brown
- *Something Beautiful* by Sharon Dennis Wyeth+
- *Something to Remember Me By* by Susan V. Bosak
- *The Keeping Quilt* by Patricia Polacco
- *The Summer My Father was Ten* by Pat Brisson

C1-a: Think about someone who was [helpful]. Tell how that experience was like the experience of _____ in the story.

Strategy for reading
As you read, look for places in the story where the character is doing things that show the trait mentioned in the question. Think about a time when you have acted the same way. The example from your life does not need to be the same kind of *experience* that the character had. It just needs to show the same *trait*.

Strategy for writing
1. Give an example from the story where the character showed a particular character trait (the one that is mentioned in the question).
2. Tell how that is like your life by giving an example that shows this same trait.

In the story, _____

_____

_____.

That is like my life because _____

_____

_____

_____.

> **C1-b: Make a personal connection. Show how something that happened in the story is like something that happened in your own life. (fiction)**

Grade level: 2-3

Teaching tips: Sometimes the objective does not specify the kind of connection students need to make. Because it is more challenging to "invent" their own connection rather than simply support a connection that has been identified for them, this objective is better suited to students beyond the early primary grades.

The challenge here is to determine a connection that has some substance to it rather than the flimsy, superficial connections students often make. (Remember the example of the dog named Shep from earlier in this chapter?) How can we help children recognize that some connections are more valuable than others?

A connection is valuable if it helps readers understand the story better. What typically leads to such deep comprehension is a thorough understanding of the characters. Hence, connecting to the *feeling* that a character had in a particular situation will allow students to connect beyond surface-level details in the plot. Good books for helping students address this objective are stories where the *feelings* of the characters are easily recognized.

One of my favorite examples of how well this notion of connecting to a feeling works came from a third-grade classroom after we read the book *Down the Road* by Alice Schertle. Micah wrote:

> "In the story Hettie felt *spontaneous* when she was running to get the eggs from the shop with her pigtails flying in the air. That is like my life because I felt *spontaneous* when my brother came home from overnight camp and I wanted to instantly play with my brother."

Before embarking on this connecting task, the class and I had brainstormed a list of "feeling" words. (See the list of feeling words on page 120 to get you started.) Someone had suggested the word *spontaneous* and we discussed its meaning. Not only did Micah use this new word immediately, he used it correctly, with a connection that showed his deeper understanding of the main character. Pretty good for a third grader!

Texts for teaching about personal connections that elicit feelings

Primary

- *Harriet, You'll Drive Me Wild!* by Mem Fox
- *My Rotten Redheaded Older Brother* by Patricia Polacco
- *Thunder Cake* by Patricia Polacco
- *Twinnies* by Eve Bunting
- *Umbrella* by Taro Yashima+
- *Wemberly Worried* by Kevin Henkes
- *When Sophie Gets Angry—Really, Really Angry...* by Molly Bang
- *Whistle for Willie* by Ezra Jack Keats+

Intermediate

- *Coming On Home Soon* by Jacqueline Woodson+
- *Down the Road* by Alice Schertle+
- *Gettin' Through Thursday* by Melrose Cooper+
- *Meet Danitra Brown* by Nikki Grimes+
- *One Green Apple* by Eve Bunting+
- *Thank You, Mr. Falker* by Patricia Polacco

FEELING WORDS

Accepted	Curious	Frantic	Incompetent	Passionate
Adored	Dazed	Frightened	Inferior	Patient
Alone	Defensive	Frustrated	Infuriated	Peaceful
Angry	Desperate	Furious	Intimidated	Proud
Anxious	Determined	Glorious	Irritated	Puzzled
Appreciated	Disappointed	Grateful	Jealous	Rejected
Ashamed	Discouraged	Gloomy	Joyful	Relaxed
Astonished	Disgusted	Grouchy	Jumpy	Relieved
Bashful	Dismayed	Grumpy	Lonely	Resentful
Bewildered	Doubtful	Guilty	Loved	Respected
Bored	Embarrassed	Hateful	Lucky	Ridiculous
Calm	Energetic	Healthy	Miserable	Safe
Carefree	Elated	Heartbroken	Mixed up	Satisfied
Cheated	Enraged	Hesitant,	Nervous	Scared
Cheerful	Envious	Hopeful	Needed	Shocked
Comfortable	Exasperated	Hopeless	Neglected	Smart
Concerned	Excited	Horrified	Offended	Tense
Confident	Exhausted	Hysterical	Out of control	Thankful
Confused	Exuberant	Helpless	Outraged	Thrilled
Content	Fearful	Impatient	Overjoyed	Trapped
Cranky	Foolish	Important	Overwhelmed	Unappreciated
Cross	Fortunate	Inadequate	Overworked	Uncomfortable

Name: _____ **Date:** _____

C1-b: Make a connection. Show how something that happened in the story is like something that happened in your own life.

<u>Strategy for reading</u>
As you are reading, pause every so often and ask yourself, "What is happening to the character right now? How does the character feel about this?" Then ask yourself, "Did I ever feel the way this character is feeling?" Think about a time when *you* felt like this character.

<u>Strategy for writing</u>
1. Tell how the character is feeling and what made him or her feel that way.
2. Tell about a time when you felt the same way.

In the story, _____ felt _____

when _____

_____ .

That is like my life because I felt _____

when _____

_____

_____ .

C1-c: Which character in the story would you like to know and why? (fiction)

Grade level: 1-3

Teaching tips: This is an objective that not only gets kids thinking about characters, but also about traits they admire in a person. Prepare your students to respond to this question by first making a list of character traits or reasons they would want to be someone's friend. Even young primary students can tell you what they like in a friend. In fact, sometimes they're quite philosophical about this. Daniel, age six, told me, "I like friends who are great at baseball like I am. Then someday we can go to the major leagues together." Daniel had apparently been doing some thinking about this and had it all figured out!

This objective encourages students to look at characters from multiple perspectives: what they say and do, the thoughts in their mind, and maybe even the way they look. Ultimately, they will need to make an inference in order to respond to this question as they will use specific details in the text combined with their own values to decide whether a character would make a worthy friend.

I think the best books for teaching this objective are those that present more than one desirable character in the same text. For example, in the primary picture book, *Mr. George Baker*, there is George and also his wife, both nice people to know but for different reasons. For older readers, consider books like *Teammates*, which is the story of the relationship between Jackie Robinson and Pee Wee Reese: *Whose character traits do you admire more?* Even picture books often have more than one "protagonist," which makes children think about the traits *most* important to them. By contrast, other books have a "hero" and a "villain." In a book like *Stand Tall Molly Lou Mellon*, for instance, not too many children will choose Ronald (the bully) over the sweet but self-confident Molly Lou!

Texts for teaching about character traits and values

Primary
- *Amazing Grace* by Mary Hoffman and Shay Youngblood+
- *Chrysanthemum* by Kevin Henkes
- *Mr. George Baker* by Amy Hest+
- *Now One Foot, Now the Other* by Tomie DePaola
- *Salt in His Shoes: Michael Jordan in Pursuit of a Dream* by Deloris and Roslyn M. Jordan+
- *The Kissing Hand* by Audrey Penn
- *The Wednesday Surprise* by Eve Bunting
- *Thunder Cake* by Patricia Polacco
- *Too Many Tamales* by Gary Soto+

Intermediate

- *Freedom Summer* by Deborah Wiles+
- *Meet Danitra Brown* by Nikki Grimes+
- *Mercedes and the Chocolate Pilot* by Margot Theis Raven
- *Minty: A Story of Young Harriet Tubman* by Alan Schroeder+
- *Night Golf* by William Miller+
- *Rotten Richie and the Ultimate Dare* by Patricia Polacco
- *Pink and Say* by Patricia Polacco+
- *Something to Remember Me By* by Susan V. Bosak
- *Teammates* by Peter Golenbock+
- *The Memory String* by Eve Bunting
- *Tomás and the Library Lady* by Pat Mora

C1-c: Which character in the story would you like to know and why?

Strategy for reading

As you read, notice where the author is telling you about different characters. Notice the kinds of things each character does, the words they speak and the thoughts they have in their mind. Do any of the characters seem like someone you would like as a friend? Why? Look for examples in the text that make you think this person would be a good friend.

Strategy for writing

1. Name the character that you would choose for a friend.
2. Explain *why* that person would be a good friend. (Does he like the same sport you like? Is the person very kind? Would she be fun to play with? There could be lots of reasons for choosing a friend.)
3. Give one or two examples from the text that *show* what he or she is like.

I would choose _____ for a friend because

_____

_____ .

Here is an example that *shows* what this person is like. _____

_____

_____ .

Here is another example that *shows* what this person is like.

_____ .

> **C1-d: Using information in the story, explain whether you would ever want to _____ . (fiction)**

Grade level: 1-3

Teaching tips: This objective often focuses on setting (time and place) or a specific event in a text: Explain whether you would want to travel west in a covered wagon like Luke in *California or Bust* (by Judith Stamper). Explain whether you would want to study snowflakes like Snowflake Bentley (in the book by the same name, by Jacqueline Martin). Why or why not? What would you like (or not like) about studying snowflakes?

This is an objective that catches many students' attention because it's about their *opinion*: The tricky part here is that students have to defend their opinion with information that comes right from the text. In the case of *Snowflake Bentley*, students can't just say, "…because I like to play in the snow." They need to reference a particular detail (or two) from the reading. For example, the student could mention that he likes photographing snowflakes (as Snowflake Bentley did). Or he could say that he thinks it would be interesting to see "the intricate patterns of snowflakes under a microscope," also in plain view in the story.

Although an event from almost any book can be used to make a personal connection, historical fiction (or nonfiction) and texts that relate to cultures other than their own are particularly promising for helping students focus on time and place. Suggestions for picture books in both of these categories are listed below.

Texts for teaching about connections to time and place

Historical perspective: primary and intermediate
- *Follow the Drinking Gourd* by Jeanette Winter+
- *California or Bust* by Judith Stamper
- *In My Momma's Kitchen* by Jerdine Nolen+
- *Little Cliff's First Day of School* by Clifton L. Taulbert+
- *Momma, Where Are You From?* by Marie Bradby+
- *She's Wearing a Dead Bird on Her Head!* by Kathryn Lasky

Stories from other distinct cultures: primary and intermediate
- *Appalachia: The Voices of Sleeping Birds* by Cynthia Rylant+
- *Children of the Earth and Sky: Five Stories about Native American Children* by Stephen Krensky+
- *Dance on a Sealskin* by Barbara Winslow+
- *Iditarod Dream* by Ted Wood+
- *Running the Road to ABC* by Denize Lauture+
- *Tea with Milk* by Allen Say+
- *When I was Young in the Mountains* by Cynthia Rylant
- *Young Cornrows Callin Out the Moon* by Ruth Forman+

C1-d: Using information in the story, explain whether you would ever want to _____ .

<u>Strategy for reading</u>
As you read, notice where the author is telling you about the event or time and place identified in the question. Think about how you would feel if you were part of this experience. Would it be fun? Would it be too hard? Would it be hard but "worth it" in the end? Why? Maybe there is another reason you would or would not want to be part of a particular experience. Be sure to notice the details of the experience as you read, so you will have evidence from the text to support your opinion.

<u>Strategy for writing</u>
1. State your opinion. (I would/would not want to…)
2. Give a reason *why* you have this opinion.
3. Use an exact detail from the text to show what you mean. Try to give a second detail, too.

I would/would not want to _____

because _____ .

Here is an example from the text that shows what I mean: _____

_____

_____ .

Here is another example from the text that shows what I mean: _____

_____

_____ .

> **C2-a: Which part of the [story/article] do you think was most important? Use information from the [story/article] and your own life to explain why you chose that part. (fiction, nonfiction)**

Grade level: 2-3

Teaching tips: Teachers are often surprised when students have difficulty finding a part of a story that is *important*. After all, *we* do it almost automatically as *we* read (find the important parts). We forget, however, that we do this with ease because we know what we're looking for. That is, we know what "counts" as important in a story: It might be where the author is giving us information about a character, where we are learning about the problem, where a character changes, or the solution to the problem. So, as we read, we search for the "right" evidence.

If we want students to be able to meet this objective, they need to know what kind of evidence to look for, too. Make a list of possible "important parts" based on stories they know well. Make sure they understand that everyone doesn't have to have the same opinion about what is important. However, they will need to defend their choice based on evidence in the text.

Sometimes this objective also asks students to connect the important event in the story to something of similar significance in their lives. Although this is a bit sophisticated for most primary-grade children, this feature can be added if appropriate.

Good texts for teaching this objective are stories with a clear turning point, an important problem, or a dramatic solution to a problem. Picture-book biographies are also good resources: *What occurred in the person's life that accounts for this person's rise to fame?*

Note that finding the most important part of a nonfiction text requires the reader to look for different kinds of evidence and is not about a *personal reaction* as much as it is about identifying *main ideas*. See objectives A1 (main idea) and D3 (what is important to a character or author) for addressing *importance* in a nonfiction text.

Texts for teaching students to find the important part of a story

Biographies and fictionalized biographies—what event(s) in the life of this person contributed to his/her success?
- *Eleanor* by Barbara Cooney
- *George Washington: A Picture Book Biography* by James Cross Giblin
- *Honest Abe* by Edith Kunhardt and Malcah Zeldis
- *Martin's Big Words* by Doreen Rappaport+
- *Mia Hamm: Winners Never Quit* by Mia Hamm

- *Minty: A Story of Young Harriet Tubman* by Alan Schroeder+
- *Salt in His Shoes: Michael Jordan in Pursuit of a Dream* by Deloris and Roslyn M. Jordan+
- *Snowflake Bentley* by Jacqueline Briggs Martin
- *Teammates* by Peter Golenbock+
- *When Marian Sang* by Pam Munoz Ryan+

Primary and intermediate books with an important problem, clear turning point, or important resolution
- *Faraway Home* by Jane Kurtz
- *Fireflies* by Julie Brinckloe
- *Gettin' Through Thursday* by Melrose Cooper+
- *Hewitt Anderson's Great Big Life* by Jerdine Nolen
- *Melissa Parkington's Beautiful, Beautiful Hair* by Pat Brisson
- *Peppe the Lamplighter* by Elisa Bartone
- *Pink and Say* by Patricia Polacco+
- *Rosa* by Nikki Giovanni+
- *Something Beautiful* by Sharon Dennis Wyeth+
- *The Bracelet* by Yoshiko Uchida+
- *The Great Kapok Tree* by Lynne Cherry
- *The Land of Many Colors* by Klamath County YMCA Preschool+
- *The Other Side* by Jacqueline Woodson+
- *The Royal Bee* by Frances Park and Ginger Park+
- *The Story of Ruby Bridges* by Robert Coles+
- *The Yellow Star* by Carmen Agra Deedy+
- *Through My Eyes* by Ruby Bridges+

C2-a: **Which part of the [story/article] do you think was *most* important? Use information from the [story/article] and your own life to explain why you chose that part.**

Strategy for reading
The most important part might be where:
- You learn something important about one of the characters
- The character changes
- The author tells about the problem
- The problem gets solved

Strategy for writing
1. Tell *what* the most important part is.
2. Tell *why* it is important.
3. Tell *how* you know it is important (a detail from the text).

I think the most important part of the story is when _____
_____
_____.

I think this is the most important part because it shows _____
_____
_____.

Here is a detail from the story that shows this: _____
_____
_____.

C2-b: Which part of this [story/article] was most interesting or surprising to you? Why? (fiction, nonfiction)

Grade level: 1-3

Teaching tips: Children love finding something that surprises them as they read. Frequently, especially at the primary level, the surprise will occur at the end of the text, though students can also be reminded that the author might surprise them at other points in the story by having a character do or say something unexpected.

For this objective, look for resources with a great "wow" factor. Some of the best texts I've discovered for teaching this objective are poems. Jack Prelutsky is the master of the "surprise ending." My favorite is his poem *New Kid on the Block*. If students are not familiar with this poem, it's perfect for teaching about surprise endings. The bully that they have pictured throughout the entire poem as a boy, turns out, in the very last line, to be a girl. In fact, in order for any text to be used effectively for teaching about a "surprising part," it must be a fresh read, not something students have seen before.

The poems for teaching this objective included in the bibliography that follows are light and humorous. Other texts with a heavier message are also useful for teaching children about how to identify a surprising part. An example would be *Goin' Somewhere Special* by Patricia C. McKissack. In this beautiful autobiographical tale, McKissack describes a day in the life of a little girl as she confronts segregation and discrimination in many forms in the pre-Civil Rights South. On this day, she strikes out on her own toward a destination that the author doesn't reveal to the reader until the final page: *"Before bounding up the steps and through the front door, 'Tricia Ann stopped to look up at the message chiseled in stone across the front facing: PUBLIC LIBRARY: ALL ARE WELCOME."*

This surprise ending becomes even more of a surprise, and more poignant as McKissack tells readers in her end note that her love of reading and writing today grew out of her love for her library as a child; it was the only place in her southern city where *all* people were free to go and therefore represented freedom.

When this objective is aligned with nonfiction or expository text, the reading and writing strategies are the same, but the kind of evidence students need to locate is different. For a nonfiction selection, the question may ask, "What is the most surprising or *interesting* part of this text?" To respond, children will want to consider what is new to them or a fact that they found startling.

Texts for all grades for finding the most interesting or surprising part

Poems—fun and funny

- *Bad Words* from "Giant Children" by Brod Bagert
- *Belinda Blue* from "Something Big Has Been Here" by Jack Prelutsky
- *Freddie* from "No More Homework! No More Tests!" by Phil Bolsta
- *I'm Disgusted with My Brother* from "New Kid on the Block" by Jack Prelutsky
- *Louder than a Clap of Thunder* from "New Kid on the Block" by Jack Prelutsky
- *My Sister Ate an Orange* from "Something Big Has Been Here" by Jack Prelutsky
- *Smart* from "Where the Sidewalk Ends" by Shel Silverstein
- *The New Kid on the Block* from "New Kid on the Block" by Jack Prelutsky
- *Today is Not a Good Day* from "A Bad Case of the Giggles" by Rebecca Kai Dotlich

Texts with a more serious surprise

- *A Picture Book of Jackie Robinson* by David A. Adler
- *Goin' Someplace Special* by Patricia C. McKissack+
- *Mr. George Baker* by Amy Hest+
- *Reflections* and *Round Trip* both by Ann Jonas
- *The Yellow Star* by Carmen Agra Deedy+
- *Too Many Tamales* by Gary Soto+

Name: _____ **Date:** _____

C2-b: Which part of this [story/article] was most interesting or surprising to you? Why?

Strategy for reading
As you read fiction, look for:
- A surprise at the end (story or poem)
- A place where a character does something you didn't expect (story)

As you read nonfiction, look for:
- Something new that you didn't know before
- A fact that startles you. (It almost seems unbelievable.)

Strategy for writing
1. Tell what was surprising.
2. Give an example/evidence from the text.
3. Tell why you were surprised.

The most surprising part of this story/article was _____

_____

_____.

Here is the evidence: _____

_____

_____.

This was surprising because _____

_____

_____.

C2-c: Did you like this story/article? Why or why not? (fiction, nonfiction)

Grade level: K-3

Teaching tips: I would argue that this is one of the most basic and important of all comprehension objectives. If we hope to raise real readers, they will need to know a whole lot about what makes a book just right for them. They will learn to choose a book for more substantial reasons than the picture on the cover, the number of pages inside, or the size of the print. Of course these may be *among* the selection criteria, but they should not be the only factors considered. By being able to articulate what they like in a book, children will be more likely to choose books with which they can connect, and they will actually finish reading those books.

Because what children like about books changes from grade to grade, I encourage teachers to talk with their students to come up with their own list of criteria for book selection. Post the chart in the library corner of your classroom, and don't forget to ask students, even informally, "Why did you choose that book? What makes that book just right for you?" Students should expect to hear that question from their teacher on a regular basis. That will help them respond to this objective more readily. Even more important, it will help them make appropriate book selections for independent reading.

The list that follows will get you and your students started as you identify criteria for choosing "just-right books" at your grade level. Note that with this objective there is no bibliography of texts provided as *any* book would be a candidate for such a list. Instead, there is a list of fiction and nonfiction genres. A good classroom library should have many genres available to match a wide variety of reading interests.

See the list on page 135 for fiction and nonfiction genres that should be represented in all classroom libraries.

A "fun" text that alerts children to the many types of texts available to them is *Read Anything Good Lately?* by Susan Allen and Jane Lindaman. It's an alphabet book that features genres: *"A, an atlas at the airport. B, a biography in bed..."* What will they think of next!

WHAT MAKES A BOOK JUST RIGHT FOR ME?
(C2-c: Why do I like—or not like—this book?)

- Is it funny?

- Is it serious?

- Is it fiction?

- Is it nonfiction?

- Is it from a genre I like?

- Is there a lot of adventure or action?

- Does it have good description?

- Does the author use interesting words?

- Does it have interesting characters?

- Does it have boy characters?

- Does it have girl characters?

- Are the characters about my age?

- Is the setting interesting to me?

- Is there a happy ending?

- Does it have an important message or lesson?

FICTION AND NONFICTION GENRES

Fiction

Drama: Stories composed in verse or prose, usually for performance, where the narrative is told through dialogue and action

Fable: Story demonstrating a useful moral or lesson, usually in which animals speak as humans

Fairy Tale: Story about fairies or other magical creatures, usually for children

Fantasy: Fiction with strange or otherworldly settings or characters; beyond the scope of reality

Fiction: Narrative literary works that come from the author's imagination and may or may not be based on facts

Folklore: The songs, stories, myths, and proverbs of a people or "folk" as handed down orally from one generation to the next

Historical Fiction: Story with fictional characters and events in a historical setting; some characters may be real

Horror: Fiction in which events evoke a feeling of dread and fear in both the characters and the reader (not suitable for early primary)

Humor: Fiction full of fun, fancy, and excitement, meant to entertain; can be contained in all genres.

Legend: Story, sometimes of a national or folk hero, which is based on fact but also includes imaginative events.

Mystery: Fiction dealing with the solution of a crime or the unraveling of secrets.

Mythology: Legend or traditional narrative, often based in part on historical events, that shows human behavior and natural phenomena through symbolism; many myths relate to the actions of the gods (may not be suitable for early primary)

Poetry: Verse and rhythmic writing with imagery that creates emotional responses

Realistic Fiction: Story that can actually happen and is true to life although the characters are not real people

Science Fiction: Story based on the imagined possibilities of science, usually set in the future or on other planets (not suitable for early primary)

Short Story: Fiction that is very brief with no subplots

Tall Tale: Humorous story with exaggerations and larger-than-life heroes who do the impossible with complete ease

Nonfiction

Biography/Autobiography: Narrative of a person's life, a true story about a real person

Essay: A short literary composition that reflects the author's outlook or point of view (not suitable for early primary)

Narrative Nonfiction: Factual information presented in a story format

Nonfiction: Any kind of informational text dealing with an actual, real-life subject

C2-c: Did you like this story/article? Why or why not?

Strategy for reading

Think about things that make a book "just right" for you. If there is a chart on the wall or a page in your reading folder with points to consider when choosing a book, be sure to look at this list. As you read the story or article, notice whether the text has some of the things (from the list or stored away in your mind) that make you like or not like this text. Be sure you can find specific examples of these things in the reading.

Strategy for writing
1. Say whether you like or do not like this story or article.
2. Give one reason why you like (or do not like) this text and show an example from the text.
3. Give a second reason why you like (or do not like) this text and show an example from the text.

I liked/did not like _____ .

One reason for this was _____

_____ .

Here is an example from the text that proves what I am saying:_____

_____

_____ .

Here is another example from the text that proves what I am saying:

_____

_____ .

C2-d: What was your first reaction to this text? Explain.
(fiction, nonfiction)

Grade level: 1-3

Teaching tips: Sometimes I worry that students are not even aware that they are *supposed* to have a reaction to a text. They are very aware that their teacher may ask them about the theme or main idea, the sequence of events, or a character. But in this age of accountability, educators are much less likely to ask, "So, how did this book make you *feel*?" Or, "What was the first thought that came to your mind after you finished this book?"

The lack of attention to this affective dimension of reading makes me sad since, above all, we want students to find personal meaning in what they read. It's that personal connection that leads to action: taking a stand on an important issue, fighting for a just cause, reading more to uncover additional answers.

In order for students to have a strong reaction to a text, they need to read something that evokes a strong emotion. The emotion can be positive or negative. But it should make them want to laugh out loud, cry, give someone "a piece of their mind," hug the main character, etc.

It is also important to provide students with the language to express these reactions: Which words on the "Feeling Words" list (page 120) are the most powerful? A few possibilities to characterize a reaction might be: *thrilled, horrified, shocked, delighted, astounded, astonished, depressed, joyful, excited, disgusted, sick, relieved,* or *peaceful*.

Texts that encourage a strong emotional reaction

Primary
- *Allie's Basketball Dream* by Barbara E. Barber
- *Big Al* by Andrew Clements
- *Coming on Home Soon* by Jacqueline Woodson
- *Mr. George Baker* by Amy Hest

Intermediate
- *Aunt Harriet's Underground Railroad in the Sky* by Faith Ringgold
- *Baseball Saved Us* by Ken Mochizuki
- *Heroes* by Ken Mochizuki
- *Stealing Home: Jackie Robinson: Against the Odds* by Robert Burleigh
- *The Story of Ruby Bridges* by Robert Coles
- *When Marian Sang* by Pam Muñoz Ryan
- *White Socks Only* by Evelyn Coleman

Name: _____ **Date:** _____

C2-d: What was your first reaction to this text? Explain.

Strategy for reading
Think about how this text makes you *feel*. As you read it, do you find yourself cheering the character on, hoping she succeeds even when it looks like she will surely fail? Do the actions of the characters make you angry? Do they create some other feeling? Think of a word that describes how you are feeling as you read this text. Find specific places in the text that cause this reaction.

Strategy for writing
1. Tell how this text makes you *feel*.
2. Tell *why* it makes you feel this way.
3. Give one or two examples that *show* what you mean.

My first reaction to this book was _____

_____.

I felt this way because _____

_____.

Here is an example that shows what I mean: _____

_____

_____

_____.

CHAPTER 9
Examining the Content and Structure of Text

This is the strand most closely aligned with critical and creative thinking. Students not only have to comprehend the literal content of a text, they need to use that information to examine the author's craft, extend the reading in some way, or demonstrate an understanding of the author's or character's customs and values. Can young children, struggling readers, and English language learners actually do this—apply basic knowledge about a text to invent a unique response? Yes, they can—with sufficient guidance and the opportunity to *talk about* their reading before *writing about* it.

Three main areas are addressed in this strand with several objectives embedded in each.

The "D" strand: Examining content and structure	
D1: Examine the author's craft	**D1-a:** Choose [2] words from paragraph ___ that help you picture the _____ . (fiction, nonfiction) **D1-b:** Choose a simile and explain why the author chose that simile. (fiction, nonfiction) **D1-c:** How did the author create humor in paragraph ___? (fiction) **D1-d:** Give an example of personification in paragraph ___ . (fiction) **D1-e:** Do you think the author made this story believable? Why or why not? (fiction)
D2: Extend the text	**D2-a:** What two questions would you like to ask the author that were not answered in this text? (fiction, nonfiction) **D2-b:** Imagine you are going to give a talk to your class about ____. What two points would you be sure to include in your speech? (nonfiction) **D2-c:** Using information in the text, write a paragraph that could have appeared in ____'s journal after _____ occurred. (fiction, nonfiction)
D3: Show that you understand what was important to an author or character	**D3-a:** How does the author/character show that _____ is important to him/her? (fiction, nonfiction) **D3-b:** How are your customs different from the customs described in this story? (fiction)

> **D1-a: Choose [2] words from paragraph ___ that help you picture the _____. (fiction, nonfiction)**

Grade level: 1-3

Teaching tips: This is the first objective in the area of author's craft. Many teachers are reluctant to address author's craft because they have so little foundation in it themselves. How many courses did *you* have in the teaching of writing as either an undergraduate or graduate student? Most teachers I know claim they have had no (or nearly no) coursework in writing, especially in the area of author's craft. In fact, they are reluctant even to define the term "author's craft."

This is unfortunate not just because it is author's craft that connects reading and writing, but because it is author's craft that makes writing—and the teaching of writing—fun. Think of author's craft as those little tricks writers employ to make their writing lively. If you enjoy reading a piece of writing, it is probably not because the topic itself is fascinating but because of the way the author wrote about the topic. There are many crafts that an author can use to get you to see things her way. One of the most basic of those crafts is *word choice*. Beginning in the earliest grades, students need to think about choosing the perfect word to convey their intended meaning—rather than simply slapping down the first word that pops into their mind. Alerting students to great word choice in the texts you read aloud can do much to model how real writers are serious about choosing words carefully.

I have noticed that the best books for modeling great word choice are not necessarily the ones with the fastest-moving plot; they are books that celebrate language through the creation of multi-sensory word images. Be sure to pause and think aloud as you come to some of these wonderful words that evoke images. How about this image from *In November* by Cynthia Rylant: "In November, the trees are standing all sticks and bones. Without their leaves, how lovely they are, spreading their arms like dancers. They know it is time to be still."

The book list that follows will get you started. When considering word choice, you may find that you seek particular authors rather than particular books. A few of the authors to whom I turn regularly for beautiful language are Cynthia Rylant, Jane Yolen, Charlotte Zolotow, Byrd Baylor, Robert Burleigh, George Ella Lyon, and Libba Moore Gray.

Texts for teaching about word choice

Primary
- *All the Colors of the Earth* by Sheila Hamanaka
- *Calling the Doves* by Juan Felipe Herrera+
- *Charlie Parker Played Be Bop* by Chris Raschka+

- *Dreamplace* by George Ella Lyon+
- *Fancy Nancy* by Jane O'Connor
- *In the Small, Small Pond* by Denise Fleming
- *Nappy Hair* by Carolivia Herron+
- *Shades of Black* by Sandra L. Pinkney
- *The Seashore Book* by Charlotte Zolotow
- *Welcome to the Green House* and *Welcome to the Sea of Sand* both by Jane Yolen

Intermediate

- *Dream: A Tale of Wonder, Wisdom & Wishes* by Susan V. Bosak
- *Harlem* by Walter Dean Myers+
- *Home Run, Hoops,* and other books by Robert Burleigh+
- *In November* by Cynthia Rylant
- *Long Night Moon* by Cynthia Rylant+
- *Scarecrow* by Cynthia Rylant
- *The Whales' Song* by Dyan Sheldon+
- *Thirteen Moons on Turtle's Back* by Joseph Bruchac+
- *Water Dance, Cloud Dance, Mountain Dance,* and other books by Thomas Locker

D1-a: Choose [2] words from paragraph _____ that help you picture
       the _____.

Strategy for reading
As you read, think about the words the author has chosen so that you get a
good picture in your mind of what he (or she) is describing. Which words
really stand out to you? Are there a few words that really help you *see* what the
author is talking about? Maybe there are words that help you use your other
senses, too: hearing, smelling, tasting, or touching. Which words are the very
BEST words? Which words are so terrific that would you like to use them in
your own writing?

Strategy for writing
   1. Find one word that helps you picture _____.
   2. Write a sentence about what that word helps you picture in your mind.
       (Try to give even more details than the author has given in the text.)
   3. Find a second word that helps you picture _____.
   4. Write a sentence about what that word helps you picture in your mind.
       (Again, try to give details about the picture in your mind.)

One word that helps me picture _____ is
_____. In my mind, I can see _____
_____.
Another word that helps me picture _____ is
_____. In my mind, I can see _____
_____.

D1-b: Choose a simile and explain why the author chose that simile. (fiction, nonfiction)

Grade level: 2-3

Teaching tips: If teachers teach any author's craft, it is likely to be similes. The definition of a simile is quite simple: a comparison that uses *like* or *as* to show the similarities between two otherwise unrelated things. (The more unlikely—but appropriate—the comparison, the more effective it is.) From an early age we point out similes to students as we read: "Oh, look, the author says the little boy is 'as hungry as a bear.' What is the simile?" Even young children can usually identify a simile on command. Explaining *why* the author chose that simile, however, is another matter—more challenging because it requires logical thinking. Students must be able to reason: *bears are often hungry and eat a lot. So if this little boy is like a bear, he must be very, very hungry.*

While this reasoning may be obvious to teachers, it is not obvious to many students, especially young children or those who struggle with reading. Taking the time to explain *why* a particular simile works will make the needed difference. Students will then begin to process similes more astutely to aid their reading comprehension. Additionally, this may help them to produce more effective similes in their own writing, too.

Similes are plentiful in literature. One genre that features similes prominently is tall tales. Take this example from "Davy Crockett" (from *American Tall Tales* by Mary Pope Osborne): "With disaster staring him in the face, Davy suddenly concentrated on grinding his own teeth—until he sounded like a hundred horsepower sawmill. Then he concentrated on growling his own growl—until he sounded like five thousand boulders tumbling down a mountainside."

The book *Quick as a Cricket* by Audrey Wood is comprised entirely of similes. It begins, "I'm as quick as a cricket, I'm as slow as a snail…" The simple text plus the endearing illustrations make this an excellent resource to introduce small children to the concept of similes.

Texts for teaching about similes

Primary
- *All the Colors of the Earth* by Sheila Hamanaka+
- *Quick as a Cricket* by Audrey Wood
- *The Seashore Book* by Charlotte Zolotow

Intermediate
- *American Tall Tales* by Mary Pope Osborne
- *The Bunyans* by Audrey Wood

Name: _____ Date: _____

D1-b: Choose a simile and explain why the author chose that simile.

<u>Strategy for reading</u>
As you read, notice where the author is comparing two things using the word *like* or *as*. For example, the author might say, "The box is as light as a feather." Or "The little girl swims like a fish." Think about why the author used that comparison: What do we know about the box if it is "as light as a feather?" What do we know about the girl if she swims "like a fish?" Decide why the author used that particular comparison.

<u>Strategy for writing</u>
1. Find a simile (a comparison using the word *like* or *as*).
2. Write a sentence that explains why the author chose to compare the first thing to the second thing. (What does it help you understand about the first thing?)

A simile I found in this story/article is _____

_____

_____.

I think the author chose this simile because it helps me understand

that _____

_____

_____.

Grade level: 3

Teaching tips: This is tricky. Note that the question does not ask students to find the humorous or funny part in a text. (They could actually *do* that with relative ease!) No, this objective asks students to identify what *makes* the passage funny. That's a little like trying to explain a joke to a person who doesn't get it.

In order to succeed with this, students have to first understand what makes something funny. Talk about this with your class. A text might be funny for many different reasons:

- Exaggeration or unlikely comparisons—such as those found in tall tales
- Made-up or silly-sounding words—Dr. Seuss is a master of this
- An amusing visual image derived from the text—like those in the *Black Lagoon* books by Mike Thaler
- A play on words or literal translation of figurative language—found in books such as *Parts* and *More Parts* by Ted Arnold or *The King Who Rained* and other books in this series by Fred Gwynne

If you create a class chart with some of these "humorous possibilities" and then refer to it as you read, children will begin to recognize why they laugh at the "funny parts."

Texts for teaching about humor in literature

Primary

- Just about any book by Dr. Seuss
- *Fortunately* by Remy Charlip
- *Parts* and *More Parts* by Tedd Arnold
- *Pigsty* by Mark Teague
- *No Jumping on the Bed* by Tedd Arnold
- *The Black Lagoon* series by Mike Thaler
- *The King Who Rained* and other books in this series by Fred Gwynne
- *That's Good! That's Bad!* by Margery Cuyler

Intermediate

- *American Tall Tales* by Mary Pope Osborne
- *Double Trouble in Walla Walla* by Andrew Clements
- *Food Fight!* by Carol Diggory Shields
- *Meanwhile, Back at the Ranch* by Trinka Hakes Noble
- *Miss Alaineus: A Vocabulary Disaster* by Debra Frasier
- *The Pig in the Spigot* by Richard Wilbur
- *Tough Cookie* by David Wisniewski

Name: _____ **Date:** _____

D1-c: How did the author create humor in paragraph ____?

Strategy for reading
As you read, notice a part that seems funny or humorous to you. Re-read that part and think about *why* it seems funny:

- Does the author exaggerate something so much that it seems silly?
- Does the author use made-up words that sound funny?
- Can you picture something in your mind that makes you laugh?
- Does the author play with words to change their meaning?

Strategy for writing
1. Write a sentence that tells *what* is funny.
2. Write a sentence that explains *why* this part is funny.

It was funny when _____   _____.   This part is funny because _____   _____   _____.

D1-d: Give an example of personification in paragraph ____. (fiction)

Grade level: 3

Teaching tips: *Personification* means that nonliving objects are given human qualities. While this may seem much too abstract for primary-grade and struggling learners, there are lots of examples from literature where this craft is employed in a manner that is very entertaining and comprehensible to children. My favorite "personification" book is *I Stink* by Kate McMullan. It is the story of a garbage truck—told from the garbage truck's point of view. In this book, the garbage truck does all the talking and children easily see what personification is all about.

There are other examples that may not *technically* qualify as personification since the narrator is "living." But the same point is made with animals that behave entirely as people (even books like the *Frog and Toad* series by Arnold Lobel) or more current books, such as *Dear Mrs. LaRue* by Mark Teague, in which the story is told in the voice of Ike, the dog, who writes letters home from the "Igor Brotweiler Canine Academy." This is a great example of personification *and* humor.

Understanding the concept of personification is important because it helps children recognize *voice* in the literary and informational texts that they read: Who is the narrator? What does this narrator care about? How would this story or article be different if it were told from another point of view?

Texts for teaching about personification

Books where animals are given human characteristics (there are thousands of books like this)

- *Arthur* books by Marc Brown
- *Berenstain Bears* books by Stan and Jan Berenstain
- *Dear Mrs. LaRue* by Mark Teague
- *Fables* by Arnold Lobel
- *Frog and Toad* series by Arnold Lobel
- *Wemberly Worried, Chrysanthemum*, and other books by Kevin Henkes

Books where inanimate objects are given a voice

- *I Stink!* by Kate McMullan
- *If a Bus Could Talk: The Story of Rosa Parks* by Faith Ringgold
- *Is that You, Winter?* by Stephen Gammell
- *The Tree That Would Not Die* by Ellen Levine

Name: _____   **Date:** _____

D1-d: Give an example of personification in paragraph _____.

Strategy for reading
As you read, notice places where an "object" (like a tree or a truck) is talking or behaving like a person. Or, it could be an animal who is talking or acting like a person. What makes this object or animal seem real? What human characteristics does it have?

Strategy for writing
1. Write a sentence that tells *what* object or animal is behaving like a person.
2. Write a sentence that tells *how* this object or animal is showing human characteristics. (Is it talking, eating people food, doing something that a person might do?)
3. Give an example that *shows* what you mean.

The object/animal that is acting like a person is _____

_____.

This object/animal is acting like a person by _____

_____.

Here is an example that shows what I mean: _____

_____

_____.

D1-e: Do you think the author made this story believable? Why or why not? (fiction)

Grade level: 1-3

Teaching tips: The problem with teaching this objective to very young children is that they have a hard time separating fantasy from reality. One time as a preschooler my daughter convinced her whole nursery school class that she had a purple kangaroo for a pet, just like the one in the story her teacher had read aloud. (We didn't have as much as a goldfish at the time.) Still, beyond the kindergarten level, students should begin to think about what is realistic in a text and what is not.

The question I invite students to ask about any text is: *Could this really happen?* We can make that question more specific: *Is the problem something that could really happen? Could events like this happen in real life? Do the characters act like, think like, talk like, and look like real people?*

By noticing the details that help them answer these questions, even young students will be able to determine if a book is based in fantasy or reality. It helps a lot if the text is one that inspires obvious connections—if the characters in the story are a lot like the children in your classroom, with comparable problems and experiences in their own lives. If the story takes place in a faraway time and place, it will be more difficult for students to decide if something could "really happen."

More advanced readers will be able to take this thinking a step further and say, "This character is *supposed* to be 'real,' but that's not the way real five-year-olds talk." Crafting characters (and problems and events) that are believable is a hallmark of good writing. If students can recognize this quality in the books they read, perhaps they will be able to make these elements believable in their own writing.

I've had fun with students as young as first grade reading fairy tales and fantasies, identifying which parts could be real and which could only exist in the imagination. In our small-group sessions, we make a game of it with students each holding their own "fantasy" and "reality" card. They read a portion of text silently, holding up the appropriate card when they have finished: Did they find an example of "fantasy" or "reality?" A few students share their evidence, going back to the text for proof. See page 152 for "Fantasy & Reality Cards" that you can duplicate and laminate for use in your own classroom.

Texts for teaching about characters, problems, and events that are believable—or not believable

Primary
Books that are very realistic
- *Allie's Basketball Dream* by Barbara E. Barber
- *Amazing Grace* by Mary Hoffman+
- *Do Like Kyla* by Angela Johnson+
- *Down the Road* by Alice Schertle+
- *Harriet, You'll Drive me Wild!* by Mem Fox
- *Too Many Tamales* by Gary Soto+
- *Twinnies* by Eve Bunting

Books where the events could never happen
- Any fairy tale
- *A Bad Case of Stripes* by David Shannon
- *Best Friends* by Steven Kellogg
- *No Jumping on the Bed* by Tedd Arnold
- *Officer Buckle and Gloria* by Peggy Rathmann
- *Stand Tall, Molly Lou Melon* by Patty Lovell
- *The Princess and the Pizza* by Mary Jane Auch
- *Where the Wild Things Are* by Maurice Sendak

Intermediate
Books that are very realistic
- *Gettin' Through Thursday* by Melrose Cooper+
- *Keepers* by Jeri Hanel Watts and Felicia Marshall
- *Meet Danitra Brown* by Nikki Grimes+
- *Some Frog!* by Eve Bunting
- *The Memory String* by Eve Bunting
- *The Summer My Father Was Ten* by Pat Brisson

Books with a combination of fantasy and reality
- Science-fiction books for children, though most of these are chapter books
- *Aunt Harriet's Underground Railroad in the Sky* by Faith Ringgold
- *Floridius Bloom and the Planet of Gloom* by Lorijo Metz
- *Probuditi!* by Chris Van Allsburg
- *Tar Beach* by Faith Ringgold
- *The Polar Express* and any other book by Chris Van Allsburg
- *The Three Questions* by Jon J. Muth
- *The Wretched Stone* by Chris Van Allsburg
- *Weslandia* by Paul Fleischman

FANTASY & REALITY CARDS

FANTASY	**FANTASY**	**FANTASY**
FANTASY	**FANTASY**	**FANTASY**
REALITY	**REALITY**	**REALITY**
REALITY	**REALITY**	**REALITY**

Name: _____ **Date:** _____

D1-e: Do you think the author made this story believable? Use details from the story to explain your answer.

Strategy for reading
Notice the evidence in the text:
1. Is the <u>setting</u> realistic?
2. Is the <u>problem</u> something that could really happen?
3. Could <u>events</u> like this happen in real life?
4. Do the <u>characters</u> act like, think like, talk like, and look like real people?
5. Try to find evidence that is really <u>important</u> to the story.

Strategy for writing
1. Write a topic sentence that tells whether the story (or events or characters) is believable.
2. Give <u>two</u> <u>important</u> examples that *show* that the story (or events or characters) is believable.

This story, _____, is/is not believable.
One reason it is/is not believable is _____
_____
_____.
Another reason is _____
_____
_____.

Grade level: K-3

Teaching tips: This *looks like* an easy objective, though sometimes our instruction in this area is a bit careless and allows students to develop bad habits. First, this question is typically asked in relation to a nonfiction text. Let's assume the topic of the article read by Joshua's third-grade class was "Our friend, the moon." After reading it, one of the questions Joshua wanted to ask the author was, "How did you become an astronomer?" On the surface, this might look like a legitimate question, but in fact, the article had nothing to do with becoming an astronomer; it was about the phases of the moon. A valid question about this article needs to focus on the specific content of the article.

The best way I know to make sure that students are asking content-specific questions is to give them text they can mark up. I tell them to underline the part of the text where they got their question. This virtually assures that the question comes straight from the reading.

While marking the text is most appropriate for older readers, even kindergarten and first-grade students can and should think about questions that a text (or author) has *not* answered, questions they are still curious about. For younger students, use a Big Book that everyone can see and in which everyone can locate the exact sentence that inspired someone's question. In many ways, identifying questions in our reading is more valuable than finding answers. It's what keeps us reading. It's what encourages us to reflect on our reading and think critically.

Almost any nonfiction book at students' developmental level is appropriate for thinking of questions to ask the author. Lots of literary texts with problems that feature societal or personal problems also work well for this.

Texts for teaching about questions to ask the author

Primary
Nonfiction

- *A Ladybug's Life* by John Himmelman
- *Bugs for Lunch* by Margery Facklam
- *Happy Birthday, Martin Luther King* by Jean Marzollo+
- *One Tiny Turtle: Read and Wonder* by Nicola Davies
- *Owls, Bats, Caves and Caverns, Giant Pandas, Groundhog Day!,* and so many more by Gail Gibbons
- *The Story of Ruby Bridges* by Robert Coles+

Fiction with important problems and themes

- *Almost to Freedom* by Vaunda Micheaux Nelson+
- *Follow the Drinking Gourd* by Jeanette Winter+
- *If a Bus Could Talk: The Story of Rosa Parks* by Faith Ringgold+
- *Nettie's Trip South* by Ann Turner+
- *Sister Anne's Hands* by Marybeth Lorbiecki+
- *The Bracelet* by Yoshiko Uchida+
- *The Lotus Seed* by Sherry Garland+
- *The Memory Coat* by Elvira Woodruff+
- *The Other Side* by Jacqueline Woodson+
- *This Is the Dream* by Diane Z. Shore and Jessica Alexander+

Intermediate

Nonfiction

- *A River Ran Wild* by Lynne Cherry
- *Christmas in the Big House: Christmas in the Quarters* by Patricia C. and Fredrick McKissack+
- *Immigrant Kids* and other books by Russell Freedman+
- *Letting Swift River Go* by Jane Yolen
- *Through My Eyes* by Ruby Bridges+
- *Weather, Volcanoes, Our Solar System* and others by Seymour Simon

Fiction with important problems and themes

- *Freedom Summer* by Deborah Wiles+
- *Baseball Saved Us* by Ken Mochizuki+
- *Heroes* by Ken Mochizuki+
- *Mama Loves Me from Away* by Pat Brisson
- *Night Golf* by William Miller+
- *Pink and Say* by Patricia Polacco+
- *Remember: The Journey to School Integration* by Toni Morrison
- *Sadako* by Eleanor Coerr+
- *Star of Fear, Star of Hope* by Jo Hoestlandt+
- *White Socks Only* by Evelyn Coleman+

Name: _____ **Date:** _____

D2-a: What two questions would you like to ask the author that are not answered in this text?

<u>Strategy for reading</u>

As you are reading, notice things that are really interesting to you. Underline these parts or put a sticky note near these places. Think what else you would like to know about these <u>specific</u> ideas. Make sure your questions come right from something the author has told you.

<u>Strategy for writing</u>

1. For your first question, tell the part in the text where you got your question. (Write down the sentence or a few words.)
2. Write the question that you have about this part of the text.
3. Find another part of the text where you got a question and write down a few words.
4. Write your question.

---

1. In the story, it tells about: _____
_____.

I would like to know _____

_____.

2. In the story, it tells about: _____
_____.

I would like to know _____

_____.

> **D2-b: Imagine you are going to give a talk to your class about _____.**
> **What two points would you be sure to include in your speech?**
> **(nonfiction)**

Grade level: 3

Teaching tips: I watch some children as they respond to this question, and it is comical. They dutifully go back to the text, find a point that looks like a main idea…and then start copying. This approach might work, except they don't know when to quit! One sentence, two sentences, an entire paragraph—they're still writing. The problem with this, of course, is that if students take this approach on a test, they will use up valuable minutes overachieving on this question and perhaps run out of time before they finish the test.

Moreover, this objective should be about more than identifying a main idea. (That objective is covered in the "A" strand.) By third grade, students should begin to think about what makes a speech effective. What makes them sit up and take note when someone is telling them about something? Little known facts can be interesting. So can comparisons that help you make a connection. A problem that someone resolved in a creative way, or a problem that still needs solving can also be interesting.

If teachers would initially approach this objective as an oral-language activity instead of a written-response question, students would more readily recognize points that are inherently more interesting. The "speeches" you snooze through probably didn't include many ideas that were noteworthy.

Books of little-known facts would be a good place to begin in addressing this objective. A particular favorite of mine is *So You Want to be President* by Judith St. George and David Small. Kids love the kinds of details in this book. Did you know that Benjamin Harrison had a goat for a pet that pulled his grandchildren around in a cart?   Other books of scientific facts and even animal rescue stories provide good material for a speech.

Texts for teaching about points to include in a speech

Primary
- *Fish Sleep But Don't Shut their Eyes* and other "Speedy Fact" books by Melvin Berger
- *The Kid's Book of Questions & Answers: Fascinating Facts about Nature, Science, Space and Much More!* by Ian Graham and Paul Sterry
- *Three Paws: The Story of Marley* by Isabela R. Presedo-Floyd

Intermediate

- *Dinner at Aunt Connie's House* by Faith Ringgold+
- *Grossology* and other books in this series by Sylvia Branzei
- *So You Want to be President, So You Want to be an Inventor,* and *So You Want to be an Explorer* by Judith St. George
- *Ten True Animal Rescues* by Jeanne Betancourt
- *The World Almanac for Kids* published annually by World Almanac

D2-b: Imagine that you are going to give a talk to your class about
_____. What two ideas would you include in your speech?

<u>Strategy for reading</u>
When you give a speech, you want everyone to be interested and to pay attention. Think about what *you* are interested in when someone tells you about something. It might be a surprising fact. It might be a comparison. It might be a problem that was hard to solve—or something else. As you are reading, watch for this kind of information. You could use it in a speech.

<u>Strategy for writing</u>
    1. Tell one idea you would include—and why you want to include it.
    2. Tell a second idea you would include—and why you want to include that, too.

One idea I would include in a speech is _____

_____.

I would tell this because _____

_____.

Another idea I would include in a speech is _____

_____.

I would tell this because _____

_____.

> **D2-c: Using information in the text, write a paragraph that could have appeared in ____'s journal after _____ occurred.**
> **(fiction, nonfiction)**

Grade level: 2-3

Teaching tips: Teaching young children or struggling readers how to meet this objective can be challenging because they need to write in a voice other than their own; they need to pretend to *be* the person about whom they are writing. Moreover, questions that ask students to produce a journal entry typically don't leave the topic completely open. Students are asked to respond to a particular incident that occurred in the text.

Teach them to begin their response with the word "I" and continue to use that pronoun throughout their whole journal entry. Asking students to write a journal entry is a way of getting them to extend the text, so they need to understand and reflect on something specific that happened. Most journal entries can be written by addressing three points: what happened, how you (the reader) feel about it, and what you will probably do next. If you can teach students to include all three of these parts, they will be able to produce consistently good journal entries.

Texts that are useful for teaching this objective are ones that include a fairly dramatic event—an event to which children are likely to have a reaction. (Be sure to identify the *most* dramatic part of the story when you ask students to write a journal entry.)

Texts for teaching about writing a journal response

Primary
- ■ *Amazing Grace* by Mary Hoffman+
- ■ *Down the Road* by Alice Schertle
- ■ *My Rotten Redheaded Older Brother* by Patricia Polacco
- ■ *Peppe the Lamplighter* by Elisa Bartone
- ■ *The Relatives Came* by Cynthia Rylant
- ■ *The Wednesday Surprise* by Eve Bunting
- ■ *Thunder Cake* by Patricia Polacco
- ■ *Tomás and the Library Lady* by Pat Mora

Intermediate
- ■ *Freedom Summer* by Deborah Wiles+
- ■ *Baseball Saved Us* by Ken Mochizuki+
- ■ *Heroes* by Ken Mochizuki+
- ■ *Melissa Parkington's Beautiful, Beautiful Hair* by Pat Brisson

- *Mercedes and the Chocolate Pilot* by Margot Theis Raven
- *My Freedom Trip* by Frances Park and Ginger Park+
- *Pink and Say* by Patricia Polacco+
- *Probuditi!* by Chris VanAllsburg
- *Sami and the Time of the Troubles* by Florence Parry Heide and Judith Heide Gilliland
- *Stealing Home: Jackie Robinson: Against the Odds* by Robert Burleigh+
- *Sweet Clara and the Freedom Quilt* by Deborah Hopkinson+
- *The Bracelet* by Yoshiko Uchida+
- *The Librarian of Basra* by Jeanette Winter+
- *The Memory String* by Eve Bunting
- *The Royal Bee* by Frances Park and Ginger Park+
- *White Socks Only* by Evelyn Coleman+

D2-c: Using information from the passage, write a paragraph that could have appeared in _____'s journal after ___ occurred.

Strategy for reading

Pretend you are the person in the story. Think about the important thing that happened and try to put it in your own words. Now think about how this would make you *feel*. Finally, think about what you would probably do next.

Strategy for writing

Remember to pretend you really are the person in the story. Start with the word "I."

1. Write a sentence that tells what happened (in your own words).
2. Tell how you feel about this.
3. Tell what you will *probably* do next.

Here is what happened: _____

_____

_____.

This made me feel _____ because _____

_____

_____.

Next, I will *probably* _____

_____

_____.

D3-a: How does the author/character show that _____ is important to him/her? (fiction, nonfiction)

Grade level: 3

Teaching tips: This is a difficult objective for children to address because it requires much higher-level, abstract thinking. This objective is not asking students to identify a character's feelings or even a character trait; it is asking that students look at the words, actions, and thoughts expressed by a character and use that information to decide what was *important* to that person. When students are asked to identify what is important to an author, this objective is even more challenging because they don't recognize that the author is speaking to them.

For questions that ask what is important to a character, choose texts about someone with a big dream. The first individual who may come to mind is Martin Luther King, Jr., but there are so many more!

For questions that ask what is important to an author, pick a book with a strong message: *What did the author want us to think about? Why did the author write this book?* If students can answer questions such as these, they will be able to tell you what is important to the author.

Texts for teaching about what is important to a character or author

Primary
- *Allie's Basketball Dream* by Barbara E. Barber (fiction)
- *Amazing Grace* by Mary Hoffman (fiction)
- *Happy Birthday, Martin Luther King* by Jean Marzollo
- *Martin's Big Words* by Doreen Rappaport (about Martin Luther King)
- *More Than Anything Else* by Marie Bradby (about Booker T. Washington)
- *Nobody Owns the Sky: The Story of Bessie Coleman* by Reeve Lindbergh
- *Salt in His Shoes*: *Michael Jordan in Pursuit of a Dream* by Deloris and Roslyn M. Jordan
- *The Librarian of Basra* by Jeanette Winter
- *Virgie Goes to School with Us Boys* by Elizabeth F. Howard

Intermediate
- *Iditarod Dream* by Ted Wood+
- *Journey to Ellis Island* by Carol Bierman
- *Letting Swift River Go* by Jane Yolen
- *Minty: A Story of Young Harriet Tubman* by Alan Schroeder
- *Running the Road to ABC* by Denize Lauture

- *Thank You, Mr. Falker* by Patricia Polacco
- *The Great Kapok Tree* by Lynne Cherry
- *The Keeping Quilt* by Patricia Polacco
- *The River Ran Wild* by Lynne Cherry
- *The Yellow Star* by Carmen Agra Deedy
- *When Marian Sang* by Pam Munoz Ryan (about Marian Anderson)

D3-a: How does the author/character show that _____ is important to him (or her)?

Strategy for reading

Important to a character: What did this person dream about? What did the person want to *do*? Find places in the reading that *show* that this person cared a lot about this special dream.

Important to the author: What did the author want us to think about? You can figure this out by noticing what the author talked about a lot. What was the author's point of view about this? What was the author for or against? Notice clues in the text that show this point of view.

Strategy for writing
1. Write a sentence that tells what this person cared (or dreamed) about.
2. Give one example from the text that *shows* this was important to the character or author.
3. Give another example from the text that *shows* this was important to the character or author.

This [character/person/author] cared a lot about _____
_____.

Something in the text that *shows* this was important to this person was: _____
_____.

Another example that *shows* this was important was: _____

_____
_____.

D3-b: How are your customs different from the customs described in this story? (fiction)

Grade level: 2-3

Teaching tips: This is not a difficult objective for students to address as long as there is an obvious contrast between students' own customs and culture and the customs and culture portrayed in the text. Stories set in a different part of the world are perfect for this: *Do people in this far-away land dress differently and eat different foods than the children in your class? Do they engage in daily activities unlike those of your students?* The illustrations in picture books give students a vivid visual image of life within distant cultures that they may not be able to picture through the author's words alone.

A word to the wise: it is certainly possible to find books that celebrate diverse cultures right within our own country, and some of these books can be used very effectively. For example, *Town Mouse, Country Mouse* by Jan Brett is a good resource for introducing even young children to the cultural differences between city life and country life. Be careful, however, about using books that feature a culture of poverty. An example of this might be *Something Beautiful* by Sharon Denis Wyeth. This is one of my all-time favorite books, and I use it with many objectives, including text-to-self connections. But I would not choose this to highlight urban culture, as the image it portrays is sometimes a negative one. The book *A Chair for My Mother* by Vera Williams would be a better choice to reinforce the many positive features of life in a city. This could be contrasted with a text such as *When I Was Young in the Mountains* by Cynthia Rylant, which depicts a young girl's love of her Appalachian heritage.

I do think it is important to use books written to showcase customs and values of a culture from a historical vantage point. Books that might fall within this category are *The Other Side* by Jacqueline Woodson and *Goin' Someplace Special* by Patricia McKissack. These books were written to give children a sense of the values (and laws) that prevailed in the pre-civil rights South.

Texts for teaching about different customs

Primary
- *All the Places to Love* by Patricia MacLachlan
- *I Hate English!* by Ellen Levine
- *Mama Panya's Pancakes: A Village Tale from Kenya* by Mary and Rich Chamberlain+
- *The Name Jar* by Yangsook Choi+
- *Too Many Tamales* by Gary Soto+
- *Town Mouse, Country Mouse* by Jan Brett
- *When I Was Young in the Mountains* by Cynthia Rylant

Intermediate

- *Appalachia: The Voices of Sleeping Birds* by Cynthia Rylant
- *Dance on a Sealskin* by Barbara Winslow
- *Eleanor* by Barbara Cooney
- *Goin' Someplace Special* by Patricia C. McKissack+
- *Momma, Where Are You From?* by Marie Bradby+
- *Seven Spools of Thread: A Kwanzaa Story* by Angela Shelf Medearis+
- *The Lotus Seed* by Sherry Garland+
- *The Other Side* by Jacqueline Woodson+
- *The Royal Bee* by Frances Park and Ginger Park+

D3-b: How are your customs different from the customs described in this story?

Strategy for reading

"Customs" are the things people of a particular region do and the way they live day-to-day, like the foods they eat, the way they celebrate special holidays, etc. As you read, look for *customs,* examples of things in the characters' or people's lives that are different from your own life. For example, do people eat different foods or wear different clothes? Do they live in different kinds of houses? Are their schools different? What about the games they play? Do they celebrate holidays that you don't celebrate? Try to find at least two or three *customs* that are different from your customs.

Strategy for writing

1. Write a sentence that tells one custom that is different for people or characters in the book. (Ex: how people eat)
2. Give one example from the text that describes the custom. (Ex: People in this story eat with chopsticks.)
3. Give an example that shows how this custom is different in *your* life. (Ex: We eat with a fork, knife, and spoon.)
4. You can repeat these steps with a second example if you wish.

One custom that is different is _____

_____.

In the book, _____

_____.

Where I live, _____

_____.

BIBLIOGRAPHY OF OBJECTIVES MATCHED TO INDIVIDUAL BOOKS

Chapters 6 through 9 contain lists of suggested books to support each objective. By contrast, the bibliography below lists books alphabetically and designates objectives appropriate for each one. As I looked at this compiled list, I chuckled a bit. It's easy to see which books are my true favorites, as m*any* objectives are listed under several of the books. I use these books often, for a wide variety of purposes. These titles would surely serve you well if you are in the market for adding to your library of children's picture books. However, every book in this bibliography has been kid-tested (and is part of my personal library)! As you add books to your own library, don't overlook texts that list a single objective. These are resources that may be new to me or that I have not had the opportunity to "test drive" as thoroughly as others.

Furthermore, you will quickly discover that aligning objectives to texts is largely a matter of personal preference. You may find yourself wondering how I could have possibly failed to notice that "Book X" is *perfect* for "Objective Y." You may also wonder why your very favorite picture book in the whole entire world isn't included in the bibliography at all. Take heart! Although this bibliography is extensive, it is not intended to be exhaustive. As you teach to specific objectives, you will want to add the books you know and love to the ones I have suggested here. And as new books are published, you will want to check them out and add some of those, too.

- *A Bad Case of Stripes* by David Shannon:
  - A1-a: What lesson does ___ learn in this story?
  - A2-d: How does ___ change in the story?
  - A3-a: Write a brief summary of this story.
  - A3-b: Summarize the main things that happened in this book.
  - B1-b: What happened at the beginning, middle, and end of the story or informational text?
  - B3-a: Prove that character/person is very ___.
  - D1-e: Do you think the author made this story believable? Explain.
- *A Chair for My Mother* by Vera B. Williams+
  - A2-b: What is ___'s main problem in the story? Give details from the story to support your answer.
  - A2-c: How did _____ solve his/her problem? Give details from the story to support your answer.
  - A3-a: Write a brief summary of this story.
  - A3-b: Summarize the main things that happened in this book.
- *A Ladybug's Life* by John Himmelman
  - D2-a: What two questions would you like to ask the author that are not answered in this text?
- *Alexander and the Terrible, Horrible, No Good, Very Bad Day* by Judith Viorst
  - B2-a: Why does the author include paragraph ___?
  - C1-a: Think about someone who was [helpful.] Tell how that experience was like the experience of ___ in the story.

- *Allie's Basketball Dream* by Barbara E. Barber
  - C2-d: What was your first reaction to this text? Why?
  - D1-e: Do you think the author made this story believable? Explain.
  - D3-a: How does the author/character show that ___ is important to him (or her)?
- *All the Colors of the Earth* by Sheila Hamanaka
  - D1-a: Choose [2] words from paragraph ___ that help you picture ___.
  - D1-b: Choose a simile and explain why the author chose that simile.
- *All the Places to Love* by Patricia MacLachlan
  - A2-e: What is the setting of the story? Give details to support your answer.
  - B1-d: Can this part of the [story/text] be described as: a definition, a description, an explanation, a conversation, an opinion, an argument, or a comparison? How do you know?
  - D3-b: How are your customs different from the customs described in this story?
- *Almost to Freedom* by Vaunda Micheaux Nelson+
  - B2-a: Why does the author include paragraph ___?
  - D2-a: What two questions would you like to ask the author that are not answered in this text?
- *Amazing Grace* by Mary Hoffman and Shay Youngblood +
  - A3-a: Write a brief summary of this story.
  - A3-b: Summarize the main things that happened in this book.
  - C1-c: Which character in the story would you like to know and why?
  - D1-e: Do you think the author made this story believable? Explain.
  - D2-c: Using information from the passage, write an entry that could have appeared in ___'s journal.
  - D3-a: How does the author/character show that ___ is important to him (or her)?
- *American Tall Tales* by Mary Pope Osborne
  - D1-b: Choose a simile and explain why the author chose that simile.
  - D1-c: How did the author create humor in paragraph ___?
- *Annabelle Swift, Kindergartner* by Amy Schwartz
  - C1-a: Think about someone who was [helpful.] Tell how that experience was like the experience of ___ in the story.
- *A Picnic in October* by Eve Bunting
  - A4-b: If the author added another paragraph to the end of the story (or article), it would <u>most likely</u> tell about _____. Use information from the story (or article) to support your answer.
  - B2-a: Why does the author include paragraph ___?
- *A Picture Book of Jackie Robinson* by David A. Adler+
  - B1-c: Compare these two characters: ___ and ___
  - C2-b: Which part of the story or article was the most surprising or interesting to you?
- *Appalachia: The Voices of Sleeping Birds* by Cynthia Rylant
  - A2-e: What is the setting of the story? Give details to support your answer.
  - C1-d: Using information from the story, explain whether you would want to ___.
  - D3-b: How are your customs different from the customs described in this story?
- *Apple Pie Tree* by Zoe Hall
  - B1-b: What happened at the beginning, middle, and end of the story or informational text?

- *A River Ran Wild* by Lynne Cherry
  - A1-c: What is this book/article mainly about?
  - A2-e: What is the setting of the story? Give details to support your answer.
  - D2-a: What two questions would you like to ask the author that are not answered in this text?
  - D3-a: How does the author/character show that ___ is important to him (or her)?
- *Arthur's Birthday* by Marc Brown (or other *Arthur* books)
  - A4-a: Predict what will happen next in the story.
  - D1-d: Give an example of personification in paragraph ___.
- *Aunt Chip and the Great Triple Creek Dam Affair* by Patricia Polacco
  - A1-b: What is the theme of this story?
  - A3-a: Write a brief summary of this story.
  - A3-b: Summarize the main things that happened in this book.
- *Aunt Harriet's Underground Railroad in the Sky* by Faith Ringgold
  - C2-d: What was your first reaction to this story? Why?
  - D1-e: Do you think the author made this story believable? Explain.
- *Baseball Saved Us* by Ken Mochizuki+
  - A2-e: What is the setting of the story? Give details to support your answer.
  - A4-b: If the author added another paragraph to the end of the story (or article), it would <u>most likely</u> tell about _____. Use information from the story (or article) to support your answer.
  - C2-d: What was your first reaction to this text? Why?
  - D2-a: What two questions would you like to ask the author that are not answered in this text?
  - D2-c: Using information from the passage, write an entry that could have appeared in ___'s journal.
- *Be My Neighbor* by Maya Ajmera & John Ivanko+
  - A1-c: What is this book/article mainly about?
- *Berenstain Bears* books by Stan and Jan Berenstain
  - D1-d: Give an example of personification in paragraph ___.
- *Best Friends* by Steven Kellogg
  - D1-e: Do you think the author made this story believable? Explain.
- *Big Al* by Andrew Clements
  - A1-b: What is the theme of this story?
  - A3-a: Write a brief summary of this story.
  - A3-b: Summarize the main things that happened in this book.
  - A4-b: If the author added another paragraph to the end of the story (or article), it would <u>most likely</u> tell about _____. Use information from the story (or article) to support your answer.
  - B1-a: What caused ___ to happen in the story?
  - B2-a: Why does the author include paragraph ___?
  - B3-a: Prove that character/person is very ___.
  - C2-d: What was your first reaction to this text? Why?
- *Bigmama's* by Donald Crews+
  - A2-e: What is the setting of the story? Give details to support your answer.
  - C1-a: Think about someone who was [helpful.] Tell how that experience was like the experience of ___ in the story.

- *Boomer's Big Surprise* by Constance McGeorge
    - A2-a: Using information in the story, write a description of how ___ felt when ____.
- *Brothers in Hope: The Story of the Lost Boys of Sudan* by Mary Williams+
    - A2-e: What is the setting of the story? Give details to support your answer.
    - B3-a: Prove that person/character is very _____.
    - C1-a: Think about someone who was [helpful.] Tell how that experience was like the experience of ___ in the story.
- *Bugs for Lunch* by Margery Facklam
    - A1-c: What is this book/article mainly about?
    - D2-a: What two questions would you like to ask the author that are not answered in this text?
- *California or Bust* by Judith Stamper
    - C1-d: Using information from the story, explain whether you would want to ___.
- *Calling the Doves* by Juan Felipe Herrera+
    - C1-a: Think about someone who was [helpful]. Tell how that experience was like the experience of _____ in the story.
    - D1-a: Choose [2] words from paragraph ___ that help you picture ___.
- *Can I Bring My Pterodactyl to School, Ms. Johnson?* by Lois Grambling
    - A3-a: Write a brief summary of this story.
    - A3-b: Summarize the main things that happened in this book.
- *Charlie Needs a Cloak* by Tomie dePaola
    - B1-b: What happened at the beginning, middle, and end of the story or informational text?
- *Charlie Parker Played Be Bop* by Chris Raschka+
    - D1-a: Choose [2] words from paragraph ___ that help you picture ___.
- *Children of the Earth and Sky: Five Stories about Native American Children* by Stephen Krensky+
    - A1-a: What lesson does ___ learn in the story?
    - C1-d: Using information from the story, explain whether you would want to ___.
- *Christmas in the Big House, Christmas in the Quarters* by Patricia C. McKissack and Fredrick McKissack+
    - A2-e: What is the setting of the story? Give details to support your answer.
    - D2-a: What two questions would you like to ask the author that are not answered in this text?
- *Chrysanthemum* by Kevin Henkes
    - A2-a: Using information in the story, write a description of how ___ felt when __.
    - A3-a: Write a brief summary of this story.
    - A3-b: Summarize the main things that happened in this book.
    - C1-c: Which character in the story would you like to know and why?
    - D1-d: Give an example of personification in paragraph ___.
- *Clever Beatrice* by Margaret Willey
    - A3-a: Write a brief summary of this story.
    - A3-b: Summarize the main things that happened in this book.

- *Coming On Home Soon* by Jacqueline Woodson+
    - A2-a: Using information in the story, write a description of how ___ felt when ___.
    - B1-a: What caused ___ to happen in the story?
    - B3-a: Prove that character/person is very ___.
    - C1-b: Make a personal connection: Show how something that happened in the story is like something that happened in your own life.
    - C2-d: What was your first reaction to this text? Why?
- *Corduroy* by Don Freeman
    - A2-a: Using information in the story, write a description of how ___ felt when ___.
    - A4-b: If the author added another paragraph to the end of the story (or article), it would <u>most likely</u> tell about _____. Use information from the story (or article) to support your answer.
    - C1-a: Think about someone who was [helpful]. Tell how that experience was like the experience of _____ in the story.
- *Dance on a Sealskin* by Barbara Winslow+
    - C1-d: Using information from the story, explain whether you would want to ___.
    - D3-b: How are your customs different from the customs described in this story?
- *Dandelion* by Don Freeman
    - A2-b: What is ___'s main problem in the story? Give details from the story to support your answer.
    - A2-c: How did ___ solve the problem? Give details from the story to support your answer.
    - A3-a: Write a brief summary of this story.
    - A3-b: Summarize the main things that happened in this book.
- *Dear Mother, Dear Daughter by Jane Yolen and Heidi Stemple*
    - B1-d: Can this part of the [story/text] be described as: a definition, a description, an explanation, a conversation, an opinion, an argument, or a comparison? How do you know?
- *Dear Mr. Blueberry* by Simon James
    - A3-c: Write a brief summary of this article/informational text.
    - A4-b: If the author added another paragraph to the end of the story (or article), it would <u>most likely</u> tell about _____. Use information from the story (or article) to support your answer.
- *Dear Mrs. LaRue* by Mark Teague
    - D1-d: Give an example of personification in paragraph ___.
- *Dear Peter Rabbit* by Alma Flor Ada
    - A3-c: Write a brief summary of this article/informational text
- *Dinner at Aunt Connie's House* by Faith Ringgold+
    - B1-d: Can this part of the [story/text] be described as: a definition, a description, an explanation, a conversation, an opinion, an argument, or a comparison? How do you know?
    - D2-b: Imagine you are going to give a talk to your class about _____. What two points would you be sure to include in your speech?

- *Do Like Kyla* by Angela Johnson+
  - A2-a: Using information in the story, write a description of how ___ felt when ___.
  - D1-e: Do you think the author made this story believable? Explain.
- *Double Trouble in Walla Walla* by Andrew Clements
  - D1-c: How did the author create humor in paragraph ___?
- *Down the Road* by Alice Schertle+
  - A1-a: What lesson does ___ learn in the story?
  - A3-a: Write a brief summary of this story.
  - A3-b: Summarize the main things that happened in this book.
  - A4-a: Predict what will happen next in the story.
  - B1-b: What happened at the beginning, middle, and end of the story or informational text?
  - C1-b: Make a personal connection: Show how something that happened in the story is like something that happened in your own life.
  - D1-e: Do you think the author made this story believable? Explain.
  - D2-c: Using information from the passage, write an entry that could have appeared in ___'s journal.
- *Dream: A Tale of Wonder, Wisdom & Wishes* by Susan V. Bosak
  - A2-d: How does ___ change in the story?
  - C1-a: Think about someone who was [helpful]. Tell how that experience was like the experience of _____ in the story
  - D1-a: Choose [2] words from paragraph ___ that help you picture ___.
- *Dreamplace* by George Ella Lyon+
  - D1-a: Choose [2] words from paragraph ___ that help you picture ___.
- *Eleanor* by Barbara Cooney
  - C2-a: Which part of the story/article do you think was the most important? Why?
  - D3-b: How are your customs different from the customs described in this story?
- *Extra! Extra! Fairy-Tale News from Hidden Forest* by Alma Flor Ada
  - A3-c: Write a brief summary of this article/informational text
- *Fables* by Arnold Lobel
  - A1-a: What lesson does ___ learn in the story?
  - D1-d: Give an example of personification in paragraph ___.
- Fairy tales
  - A1-b: What is the theme of this story?
- *Fancy Nancy* by Jane O'Connor
  - D1-a: Choose [2] words from paragraph ___ that help you picture ___.
- *Faraway Home* by Jane Kurtz
  - A2-a: Using information in the story, write a description of how ___ felt when __.
  - C2-a: Which part of the story/article do you think was the most important? Why?
- *Firefighters* by Christopher Mitten
  - A1-c: What is this book/article mainly about?
  - B1-d: Can this part of the [story/text] be described as: a definition, a description, an explanation, a conversation, an opinion, an argument, or a comparison? How do you know?

- *Fireflies* by Julie Brinckloe
    - A2-a: Using information in the story, write a description of how ___ felt when __.
    - A4-b: If the author added another paragraph to the end of the story (or article), it would <u>most likely</u> tell about _____. Use information from the story (or article) to support your answer.
    - C2-a: Which part of the story/article do you think was the most important? Why?
- *Fish Sleep But Don't Shut their Eyes* and other "Speedy Fact" books by Melvin Berger
    - D2-b: Imagine that you are giving a talk to your class. What two ideas would you include in your speech?
- *Floridius Bloom and the Planet of Gloom* by Lorijo Metz
    - B3-a: Prove that character/person is very ___.
    - D1-e: Do you think the author made this story believable? Explain.
- *Follow the Drinking Gourd* by Jeanette Winter+
    - B1-b: What happened at the beginning, middle, and end of the story or informational text?
    - C1-d: Using information from the story, explain whether you would want to ___.
    - D2-a: What two questions would you like to ask the author that are not answered in this text?
- *Food Fight!* by Carol Diggory Shields
    - D1-c: How did the author create humor in paragraph ___?
- *Fortunately* by Remy Charlip
    - D1-c: How did the author create humor in paragraph ___?
- *Frederick* by Leo Lionni
    - A3-a: Write a brief summary of this story.
    - A3-b: Summarize the main things that happened in this book.
    - B1-c: Compare these two characters: ___ and ___
- *Freedom School, Yes!* by Amy Littlesugar+
    - A1-a: What lesson does ___ learn in the story?
    - A2-d: How does ___ change in the story?
- *Freedom Summer* by Deborah Wiles+
    - A1-b: What is the theme of this story?
    - A4-b: If the author added another paragraph to the end of the story (or article), it would <u>most likely</u> tell about _____. Use information from the story (or article) to support your answer.
    - B1-a: What caused ___ to happen in the story?
    - C1-c: Which character in the story would you like to know and why?
    - D2-a: What two questions would you like to ask the author that are not answered in this text?
    - D2-c: Using information from the passage, write an entry that could have appeared in __'s journal.
- *Frog and Toad* series by Arnold Lobel
    - D1-d: Give an example of personification in paragraph ___.
- *From Caterpillar to Butterfly* by Deborah Heiligman
    - B1-b: What happened at the beginning, middle, and end of the story or informational text?

- *From Seed to Plant* by Gail Gibbons
  - B1-b: What happened at the beginning, middle, and end of the story or informational text?
  - B1-d: Can this part of the [story/text] be described as: a definition, a description, an explanation, a conversation, an opinion, an argument, or a comparison? How do you know?
- *From Tadpole to Frog* by Wendy Pfeffer
  - B1-b: What happened at the beginning, middle, and end of the story or informational text?
- *George Washington: A Picture Book Biography* by James Cross Giblin
  - A1-c: What is this book/article mainly about?
  - C2-a: Which part of the story/article do you think was the most important? Why?
- *Gettin' Through Thursday* by Melrose Cooper+
  - B1-b: What happened at the beginning, middle, and end of the story or informational text?
  - C1-b: Make a personal connection: Show how something that happened in the story is like something that happened in your own life.
  - C2-a: Which part of the story/article do you think was the most important? Why?
  - D1-e: Do you think the author made this story believable? Explain.
- *Goin' Someplace Special* by Patricia C. McKissack+
  - B2-a: Why does the author include paragraph ___?
  - C2-b: Which part of this text was most interesting or surprising to you? Why?
  - D3-b: How are your customs different from the customs described in this story?
- *Grossology* and other books in this series by Sylvia Branzei
  - D2-b: Imagine that you are giving a talk to your class. What two ideas would you include in your speech?
- *Happy Birthday, Martin Luther King* by Jean Marzollo+
  - D2-a: What two questions would you like to ask the author that are not answered in this text?
  - D3-a: How does the author/character show that ___ is important to him (or her)?
- *Harlem* by Walter Dean Myers+
  - D1-a: Choose [2] words from paragraph ___ that help you picture ___.
- *Harriet, You'll Drive me Wild!* by Mem Fox
  - C1-b: Make a personal connection. Show how something that happened in the story is like something that happened in your own life.
  - D1-e: Do you think the author made this story believable? Explain.
- *Heroes* by Ken Mochizuki+
  - A2-e: What is the setting of the story? Give details to support your answer.
  - A4-b: If the author added another paragraph to the end of the story (or article), it would <u>most likely</u> tell about _____. Use information from the story (or article) to support your answer.
  - C2-d: What was your first reaction to this text? Why?
  - D2-a: What two questions would you like to ask the author that are not answered in this text?
  - D2-c: Using information from the passage, write an entry that could have appeared in ___'s journal.

- *Hewitt Anderson's Great Big Life* by Jerdine Nolen
  - A1-b: What is the theme of this story?
  - B2-a: Why does the author include paragraph ___?
  - C2-a: Which part of the story/article do you think was the most important? Why?
- *Hey, Little Ant* by Phillip M. and Hannah Hoose
  - A4-a: Predict what will happen next in the story.
  - B1-d: Can this part of the [story/text] be described as: a definition, a description, an explanation, a conversation, an opinion, an argument, or a comparison? How do you know?
- *Honest Abe* by Edith Kunhardt and Malcah Zeldis
  - C2-a: Which part of the story/article do you think was the most important? Why?
- *Hoops, Home Run,* and others by Robert Burleigh+
  - B1-d: Can this part of the [story/text] be described as: a definition, a description, an explanation, a conversation, an opinion, an argument, or a comparison? How do you know?
  - D1-a: Choose [2] words from paragraph ___ that help you picture ___.
- *Hooway for Wodney Wat* by Helen Lester
  - A2-b: What is ___'s main problem in the story? Give details from the story to support your answer.
  - A2-c: How did ___ solve the problem? Give details from the story to support your answer.
- *How is a Crayon Made?* By Oz Charles
  - B1-b: What happened at the beginning, middle, and end of the story or informational text?
  - B1-d: Can this part of the [story/text] be described as: a definition, a description, an explanation, a conversation, an opinion, an argument, or a comparison? How do you know?
- *How a House is Built* by Gail Gibbon
  - B1-d: Can this part of the [story/text] be described as: a definition, a description, an explanation, a conversation, an opinion, an argument, or a comparison? How do you know?
- *I Hate English!* by Ellen Levine+
  - A2-d: How does ___ change in the story?
  - D3-b: How are your customs different from the customs described in this story?
- *Iditarod Dream* by Ted Wood+
  - C1-d: Using information from the story, explain whether you would want to ___.
  - D3-a: How does the author/character show that _____ is important to him/her?
- *If a Bus Could Talk: The Story of Rosa Parks* by Faith Ringgold
  - D1-d: Give an example of personification in paragraph ___.
  - D2-a: What two questions would you like to ask the author that were not answered in this text?
- *If You Lived in Colonial Times* by Ann McGovern
  - A1-c: What is this book/article mainly about?
  - B3-b: Which facts show that ___?

- *If You Traveled on the Underground Railroad* by Ellen Levine (and many other titles, all published by Scholastic)
  - A1-c: What is this book/article mainly about?
  - B3-b: Which facts show that ___?
- *If You Traveled West in a Covered Wagon* by Ellen Levine and other books in this series published by Scholastic are excellent resources for teaching main idea.
  - A1-c: What is this book/article mainly about?
  - B3-b: Which facts show that ___?
- *Immigrant Kids* and other books by Russell Freedman+
  - A1-c: What is this book/article mainly about?
  - B3-b: Which facts show that ___?
  - D2-a: What two questions would you like to ask the author that are not answered in this text?
- *In My Momma's Kitchen* by Jerdine Nolen+
  - C1-a: Think about someone who was [helpful.] Tell how that experience was like the experience of ___ in the story.
  - C1-d: Using information from the story, explain whether you would want to ___.
- *In November and Scarecrow by Cynthia Rylant*
  - B1-d: Can this part of the [story/text] be described as: a definition, a description, an explanation, a conversation, an opinion, an argument, or a comparison? How do you know?
  - D1-a: Choose [2] words from paragraph ___ that help you picture ___.
- *In the Small, Small Pond* by Denise Fleming
  - D1-a: Choose [2] words from paragraph ___ that help you picture ___.
- *Ira Sleeps Over* by Bernard Waber
  - A2-b: What is ___'s main problem in the story? Give details from the story to support your answer.
  - A2-c: How did ___ solve the problem? Give details from the story to support your answer.
  - C1-a: Think about someone who was [helpful.] Tell how that experience was like the experience of ___ in the story.
- *Is that You, Winter?* by Stephen Gammell
  - B1-d: Can this part of the [story/text] be described as: a definition, a description, an explanation, a conversation, an opinion, an argument, or a comparison? How do you know?
  - D1-d: Give an example of personification in paragraph ___.
- *I Stink!* by Kate McMullan
  - D1-d: Give an example of personification in paragraph ___.
- *Is Your Mama a Llama?* by Deborah Guarino
  - A4-a: Predict what will happen next in the story.
- *Joseph had a Little Overcoat* by Simms Taback
  - A2-b: What is ___'s main problem in the story? Give details from the story to support your answer.
  - A2-c: How did ___ solve the problem? Give details from the story to support your answer.
- *Journey to Ellis Island* by Carol Bierman
  - A1-c: What is this book/article mainly about?
  - B3-b: Which facts show that ___?

D3-a: How does the author/character show that ___ is important to him (or her)?

- *Julius, the Baby of the World* by Kevin Henkes
    B1-a: What caused ___ to happen in the story?
- *Keep Climbing, Girls* by Beah E. Richards+
    A1-b: What is the theme of this story?
- *Keepers* by Jeri Hanel Watts and Felicia Marshall
    A2-b: What is _____'s main problem in the story? Give details from the story to support your answer. (fiction)
    A2-c: How did ___ solve the problem? Give details from the story to support your answer.
    D1-e: Do you think the author made this story believable? Explain.
- *Kindergarten Kids* by Ellen B. Senisi
    A1-c: What is this book/article mainly about?
- *Kitten's First Full Moon* by Kevin Henkes
    A2-a: Using information in the story, write a description of how ___ felt when __.
    A3-a: Write a brief summary of this story.
    A3-b: Summarize the main things that happened in this book.
    B1-b: What happened at the beginning, middle, and end of the story or informational text?
- *Koala Lou* by Mem Fox
    A1-b: What is the theme of this story?
    A3-a: Write a brief summary of this story.
    A3-b: Summarize the main things that happened in this book.
- *Leo the Late Bloomer* by Robert Kraus
    A1-b: What is the theme of this story?
    A2-d: How did ___ change from the beginning to the end of the story?
- *Letting Swift River Go* by Jane Yolen
    A2-e: What is the setting of the story? Give details to support your answer.
    D2-a: What two questions would you like to ask the author that are not answered in this text?
    D3-a: How does the author/character show that ___ is important to him (or her)?
- *Lincoln: A Photobiography, The Wright Brothers,* and others by Russell Freedman
    A1-c: What is this book/article mainly about?
    B3-b: Which facts show that ___?
- *Little Cliff's First Day of School* by Clifton L. Taulbert+
    C1-d: Using information from the story, explain whether you would want to ___.
- *Long Night Moon* by Cynthia Rylant+
    A2-e: What is the setting of this story? Give details to support your answer.
    D1-a: Choose [2] words from paragraph ___ that help you picture ___.
- *Lunch* by Denise Fleming
    A4-a: Predict what will happen next in the story.
- *Mama Loves Me from Away* by Pat Brisson
    A2-a: Using information in the story, write a description of how ___ felt when __.
    B1-a: What caused ___ to happen in the story?
    D2-a: What two questions would you like to ask the author that are not answered in this text?

■ *Mama Panya's Pancakes: A Village Tale from Kenya* by Mary and Rich Chamberlin+

    A2-e: What is the setting of the story? Give details to support your answer.

    D3-b: How are your customs different from the customs described in this story?

■ *Martin's Big Words* by Doreen Rappaport+

    C2-a: Which part of the story/article do you think was the most important? Why?

    D3-a: How does the author/character show that ___ is important to him (or her)?

■ *Me, All Alone, at the End of the World* by M.T. Anderson

    A2-d: How does ___ change in the story?

    B2-a: Why does the author include paragraph ___?

■ *Meanwhile, Back at the Ranch* by Trinka Hakes Noble

    D1-c: How did the author create humor in paragraph ___?

■ *Meet Danitra Brown* by Nikki Grimes+

    A2-a: Using information in the story, write a description of how ___ felt when __.

    B1-c: Compare these two characters: ___ and ___.

    C1-b: Make a personal connection: Show how something that happened in the story is like something that happened in your own life.

    C1-c: Which character in the story would you like to know and why?

    D1-e: Do you think the author made this story believable? Explain.

■ *Melissa Parkington's Beautiful, Beautiful Hair* by Pat Brisson

    A1-a: What lesson does ___ learn in the story?

    A2-d: How does ___ change in the story?

    A3-a: Write a brief summary of this story.

    A3-b: Summarize the main things that happened in this book.

    B1-b: What happened at the beginning, middle, and end of the story or informational text?

    B3-a: Prove that character/person is very ___.

    C1-a: Think about someone who was [helpful.] Tell how that experience was like the experience of ___ in the story.

    C2-a: Which part of the story/article do you think was the most important? Why?

    D2-c: Using information from the passage, write an entry that could have appeared in ___'s journal.

■ *Mercedes and the Chocolate Pilot* by Margot Theis Raven+

    A2-e: What is the setting of the story? Give details to support your answer.

    C1-c: Which character in the story would you like to know and why?

    D2-c: Using information from the passage, write an entry that could have appeared in ___'s journal.

■ *Mia Hamm: Winners Never Quit* by Mia Hamm

    B2-a: Why does the author include paragraph ___?

    B3-a: Prove that character/person is very ___.

    C2-a: Which part of the story/article do you think was the most important? Why?

■ *Minty: A Story of Young Harriet Tubman* by Alan Schroeder+

    A2-a: Using information in the story, write a description of how ___ felt when __.

    B1-d: Can this part of the [story/text] be described as: a definition, a description, an explanation, a conversation, an opinion, an argument, or a comparison?

How do you know?

  B2-a: Why does the author include paragraph ___?

  C1-c: Which character in the story would you like to know and why?

  C2-a: Which part of the story/article do you think was the most important? Why?

  D3-a: How does the author/character show that ___ is important to him (or her)?

■ *Miss Alaineus: A Vocabulary Disaster* by Debra Frasier

  D1-c: How did the author create humor in paragraph ___?

■ *Miss Bridie Chose a Shovel* by Leslie Connor

  B1-b: What happened at the beginning, middle, and end of the story or informational text?

  B3-a: Prove that character/person is very ___.

■ *Miss Rumphius* by Barbara Cooney

  A4-b: If the author added another paragraph to the end of the story (or article), it would <u>most likely</u> tell about _____. Use information from the story (or article) to support your answer.

  B1-a: What caused ___ to happen in the story?

■ *Momma, Where Are You From?* by Marie Bradby+

  C1-d: Using information from the story, explain whether you would want to ___.

  D3-b: How are your customs different from the customs described in this story?

■ *More than Anything Else* by Marie Bradby+

  B2-a: Why does the author include paragraph ___?

  B3-a: Prove that character/person is very ___.

  D3-a: How does the author/character show that ___ is important to him (or her)?

■ *Mr. George Baker* by Amy Hest+

  B2-a: Why does the author include paragraph ___?

  C1-c: Which character in the story would you like to know and why?

  C2-b: Which part of this text was most interesting or surprising to you? Why?

  C2-d: What was your first reaction to this text? Why?

■ *My Dog is Lost* by Ezra Jack Keats

  B1-a: What caused ___ to happen in the story?

■ *My Dream of Martin Luther King* by Faith Ringgold+

  B1-d: Can this part of the [story/text] be described as: a definition, a description, an explanation, a conversation, an opinion, an argument, or a comparison? How do you know?

■ *My Freedom Trip: A Child's Escape from North Korea* by Frances Park and Ginger Park+

  A2-e: What is the setting of the story? Give details to support your answer.

  D2-c: Using information from the passage, write an entry that could have appeared in ___'s journal.

■ *My Rotten Redheaded Older Brother* by Patricia Polacco

  A2-a: Using information in the story, write a description of how ___ felt when __.

  A2-d: How does ___ change in the story?

  C1-b: Make a personal connection: Show how something that happened in the story is like something that happened in your own life.

  D2-c: Using information from the passage, write an entry that could have appeared in ___'s journal.

- *Nappy Hair* by Carolivia Herron+
  - D1-a: Choose [2] words from paragraph ___ that help you picture ___.
- *Nettie's Trip South* by Ann Turner+
  - A2-a: Using information in the story, write a description of how ___ felt when __.
  - B1-a: What caused ___ to happen in the story?
  - D2-a: What two questions would you like to ask the author that are not answered in this text?
- *Night Golf* by William Miller+
  - C1-c: Which character in the story would you like to know and why?
  - D2-a: What two questions would you like to ask the author that are not answered in this text?
- *Nobody Owns the Sky: The Story of Bessie Coleman* by Reeve Lindbergh+
  - B1-d: Can this part of the [story/text] be described as: a definition, a description, an explanation, a conversation, an opinion, an argument, or a comparison? How do you know?
  - B2-a: Why does the author include paragraph ___?
  - B3-a: Prove that character/person is very ___.
  - D3-a: How does the author/character show that ___ is important to him (or her)?
- *No Jumping on the Bed* by Tedd Arnold
  - D1-c: How did the author create humor in paragraph ___?
  - D1-e: Do you think the author made this story believable? Explain.
- *Now One Foot, Now the Other* by Tomie dePaola
  - C1-a: Think about someone who was [helpful.] Tell how that experience was like the experience of ___ in the story.
  - C1-c: Which character in the story would you like to know and why?
- *Odd Boy Out: Young Albert Einstein* by Don Brown
  - A1-a: What lesson does ___ learn in the story?
  - C1-a: Think about someone who was [helpful.] Tell how that experience was like the experience of ___ in the story.
- *Officer Buckle and Gloria* by Peggy Rathmann
  - A2-b: What is ___'s main problem in the story? Give details from the story to support your answer.
  - A2-c: How did ___ solve the problem? Give details from the story to support your answer.
  - B1-b: What happened at the beginning, middle, and end of the story or informational text?
  - D1-e: Do you think the author made this story believable? Explain.
- *One Green Apple* by Eve Bunting+
  - A2-a: Using information in the story, write a description of how ___ felt when __.
  - C1-b: Make a connection: Show how something that happened in the story is like something that happened in your own life.
- *One Tiny Turtle: Read and Wonder* by Nicola Davies
  - B1-b: What happened at the beginning, middle, and end of the story or informational text?
  - B1-d: Can this part of the [story/text] be described as: a definition, a description, an explanation, a conversation, an opinion, an argument, or a comparison? How do you know?

D2-a: What two questions would you like to ask the author that are not answered in this text?

- *Owls, Bats, Caves and Caverns, Giant Pandas, Groundhog Day!,* and so many more by Gail Gibbons

    D2-a: What two questions would you like to ask the author that are not answered in this text?

- *Owen and Mzee: The True Story of a Remarkable Friendship* by Isabella Hatkoff, Craig Hatkoff, and Dr. Paula Kahumbu

    A2-e: What is the setting of the story? Give details to support your answer.

    B1-d: Can this part of the [story/text] be described as: a definition, a description, an explanation, a conversation, an opinion, an argument, or a comparison? How do you know?

- *Parts* and *More Parts* by Tedd Arnold

    D1-c: How did the author create humor in paragraph ___?

- *Peppe the Lamplighter* by Elisa Bartone

    A1-b: What is the theme of this story?

    A2-d: How does ___ change in the story?

    B2-a: Why does the author include paragraph ___?

    C2-a: Which part of the story/article do you think was the most important? Why?

    D2-c: Using information from the passage, write an entry that could have appeared in ___'s journal.

- *Pigsty* by Mark Teague

    C1-a: Think about someone who was [helpful.] Tell how that experience was like the experience of ___ in the story.

    D1-c: How did the author create humor in paragraph ___?

- *Pink and Say* by Patricia Polacco+

    C1-c: Which character in the story would you like to know and why?

    C2-a: Which part of the story/article do you think was the most important? Why?

    D2-a: What two questions would you like to ask the author that are not answered in this text?

    D2-c: Using information from the passage, write an entry that could have appeared in ___'s journal.

- *Princess Penelope's Parrot* by Helen Lester

    A1-a: What lesson does ___ learn in the story?

    A2-d: How does ___ change in the story?

    B3-a: Prove that character/person is very ___.

- *Probuditi!* by Chris VanAllsburg

    A4-a: Predict what will happen next in this story.

    D1-e: Do you think the author made this story believable?

    D2-c: Using information from the passage, write an entry that could have appeared in ___'s journal.

- *Quick as a Cricket* by Audrey Wood

    D1-b: Choose a simile and explain why the author chose that simile.

- *Reflections* and *Round Trip* both by Ann Jonas

    C2-b: Which part of this text was most interesting or surprising to you? Why?

- *Remember: The Journey to School Integration* by Toni Morrison
  - B2-a: Why does the author include paragraph ___?
  - D2-a: What two questions would you like to ask the author that are not answered in this text?
- *Ricardo's Day* by George Ancona+
  - A1-c: What is this book/article mainly about?
- *Rosa* by Nikki Giovanni+
  - A1-a: What lesson does ___ learn in the story?
  - C2-a: Which part of the story/article do you think was the most important? Why?
- *Rotten Richie and the Ultimate Dare* by Patricia Polacco
  - A3-a: Write a brief summary of this story.
  - A3-b: Summarize the main things that happened in this book.
  - B1-a: What caused ___ to happen in the story?
  - C1-c: Which character in the story would you like to know and why?
- *Running the Road to ABC* by Denize Lauture+
  - C1-d: Using information from the story, explain whether you would want to ___.
  - D3-a: How does the author/character show that _____ is important to him/her?
- *Sadako* by Eleanor Coerr+
  - A3-a: Briefly summarize this story.
  - A3-b: Summarize the main things that happened in this book.
  - D2-a: What two questions would you like to ask the author that are not answered in this text?
- *Salt in His Shoes: Michael Jordan in Pursuit of a Dream* by Deloris and Roslyn M. Jordan+
  - B1-b: What happened at the beginning, middle, and end of the story or informational text?
  - B3-a: Prove that character/person is very ___.
  - C1-c: Which character in the story would you like to know and why?
  - C2-a: Which part of the story/article do you think was the most important? Why?
  - D3-a: How does the author/character show that ___ is important to him (or her)?
- *Sami and the Time of the Troubles* by Florence Parry Heide and Judith Heide Gilliland+
  - A2-e: What is the setting of the story? Give details to support your answer.
  - D2-c: Using information in the text, write a paragraph that could have appeared in ____'s journal after _____ occurred.
- *Scarecrow* by Cynthia Rylant
  - A2-e: What is the setting of this story? Give details to support your answer.
  - D1-a: Choose [2] words from paragraph ___ that help you picture ___.
- *Seven Spools of Thread: A Kwanzaa Story* by Angela Shelf Medearis+
  - D3-b: How are your customs different from the customs described in this story?
- *Shades of Black* by Sandra L. Pinkney
  - D1-a: Choose [2] words from paragraph ___ that help you picture ___.
- *She's Wearing a Dead Bird on Her Head!* by Kathryn Lasky
  - A2-d: How does ___ change in the story?.
  - C1-d: Using information from the story, explain whether you would want to ___.

- *Sister Anne's Hands* by Marybeth Lorbiecki+
    - A1-b: What is the theme of this story?
    - B1-a: What caused ___ to happen in the story?
    - D2-a: What two questions would you like to ask the author that are not answered in this text?
- *Snowflake Bentley* by Jacqueline Briggs Martin
    - B2-a: Why does the author include paragraph ___?
    - C2-a: Which part of the story/article do you think was the most important? Why?
- *Some Frog!* by Eve Bunting
    - A2-a: Using information in the story, write a brief description of how _____ felt when ___.
    - D1-e: Do you think the author made this story believable? Explain.
- *Someday a Tree* by Eve Bunting
    - B1-a: What caused ___ to happen in the story?
- *Something Beautiful* by Sharon Dennis Wyeth+
    - A1-b: What is the theme of this story?
    - B2-a: Why does the author include paragraph ___?
    - C1-a: Think about someone who was [helpful.] Tell how that experience was like the experience of ___ in the story.
    - C2-a: Which part of the story/article do you think was the most important? Why?
- *Something to Remember Me By* by Susan V. Bosak
    - C1-a: Think about someone who was [helpful.] Tell how that experience was like the experience of ___ in the story.
    - C1-c: Which character in the story would you like to know and why?
- *So You Want to be President*, *So You Want to be an Inventor,* and *So You Want to be an Explorer* by Judith St. George
    - D2-b: Imagine that you are giving a talk to your class. What two ideas would you include in your speech?
- *Stand Tall, Molly Lou Melon* by Patty Lovell
    - A1-a: What lesson does ___ learn in the story?
    - A2-d: How does ___ change in the story?
    - A4-b: If the author added another paragraph to the end of the story (or article), it would most likely tell about _____. Use information from the story (or article) to support your answer.
    - B1-c: Compare these two characters: ___ and ___
    - B3-a: Prove that character/person is very ___.
    - D1-e: Do you think the author made this story believable? Explain.
- *Star of Fear, Star of Hope* by Jo Hoestlandt+
    - A2-a: Using information in the story, write a brief description of how _____ felt when ___.
    - D2-a: What two questions would you like to ask the author that are not answered in this text?
- *Stealing Home: Jackie Robinson: Against the Odds* by Robert Burleigh
    - C2-d: What was your first reaction to this text? Why?
    - D2-c: Using information from the passage, write an entry that could have appeared in __'s journal after ___ occurred.

- *Stellaluna* by Janell Cannon
    - A3-a: Write a brief summary of this story.
    - A3-b: Summarize the main things that happened in this book.
- *Sweet Clara and the Freedom Quilt* by Deborah Hopkinson+
    - B1-a: What caused ___ to happen in the story?
    - B1-d: Can this part of the [story/text] be described as: a definition, a description, an explanation, a conversation, an opinion, an argument, or a comparison? How do you know?
    - D2-c: Using information from the passage, write an entry that could have appeared in ___'s journal after ___ occurred.
- *Tacky the Penguin* by Helen Lester
    - A1-b: What is the theme of this story?
    - A3-a: Write a brief summary of this story.
    - A3-b: Summarize the main things that happened in this book.
    - B1-c: Compare these two characters: ___ and ___
    - B3-a: Prove that character/person is very ___.
- *Talkin' About Bessie: The Story of Aviator Elizabeth Coleman* by Nikki Grimes+
    - B1-d: Can this part of the [story/text] be described as: a definition, a description, an explanation, a conversation, an opinion, an argument, or a comparison? How do you know?
    - B2-a: Why does the author include paragraph ___?
- *Tar Beach* by Faith Ringgold
    - A1-b: What is the theme of this story?
    - D1-e: Do you think the author made this story believable? Explain.
- *Tea with Milk* by Allen Say+
    - B1-b: What happened at the beginning, middle, and end of the story or informational text?
    - B2-a: Why does the author include paragraph ___?
    - B3-a: Prove that character/person is very ___.
    - C1-d: Using information from the story, explain whether you would want to ___.
- *Teammates* by Peter Golenbock+
    - B1-c: Compare these two characters: ___ and ___
    - C1-c: Which character in the story would you like to know and why?
    - C2-a: Which part of the story/article do you think was the most important? Why?
- *Tell Me a Story Mama* by Angela Johnson+
    - C1-a: Think about someone who was [helpful.] Tell how that experience was like the experience of ___ in the story.
- *Ten True Animal Rescues* by Jeanne Betancourt
    - D2-b: Imagine that you are giving a talk to your class. What two ideas would you include in your speech?
- *Thank You, Mr. Falker* by Patricia Polacco
    - A2-a: Using information in the story, write a description of how ___ felt when ___.
    - C1-b: Make a personal connection: Show how something that happened in the story is like something that happened in your own life.
    - D3-a: How does the author/character show that ___ is important to him (or her)?

- *That's Good! That's Bad!* by Margery Cuyler
    - D1-c: How did the author create humor in paragraph ___?
- *The Black Lagoon* series by Mike Thaler
    - D1-c: How did the author create humor in paragraph ___?
- *The Bunyans* by Audrey Wood
    - D1-b: Choose a simile and explain why the author chose that simile.
- *The Bracelet* by Yoshiko Uchida+
    - A2-e: What is the setting of the story? Give details to support your answer.
    - C2-a: Which part of the story/article do you think was the most important? Why?
    - D2-a: What two questions would you like to ask the author that are not answered in this text?
    - D2-c: Using information from the passage, write an entry that could have appeared in ___'s journal after ___ occurred.
- *The Bus Ride* by William Miller+
    - A2-b: What is ___'s main problem in the story? Give details from the story to support your answer.
    - A2-c: How did ___ solve the problem? Give details from the story to support your answer.
- *The Cats in Krasinski Square* by Karen Hesse+
    - A2-b: What is ___'s main problem in the story? Give details from the story to support your answer.
    - A2-c: How did ___ solve the problem? Give details from the story to support your answer.
- *The Day Jimmy's Boa Ate the Wash* by Trinka Hakes Noble
    - A4-a: Predict what will happen next in the story.
- *The Emperor Lays an Egg* by Brenda Z. Guiberson
    - B1-b: What happened at the beginning, middle, and end of the story or informational text?
    - B3-b: Which facts show that ___?
- *The Gigantic Turnip* by Aleksei Tolstoy
    - A3-a: Write a brief summary of this story.
    - A3-b: Summarize the main things that happened in this book.
- *The Great Kapok Tree* by Lynne Cherry+
    - A2-e: What is the setting of the story? Give details to support your answer.
    - C2-a: Which part of the story/article do you think was the most important? Why?
    - D3-a: How does the author/character show that ___ is important to him (or her)?
- *The Hello, Goodbye Window* by Norton Juster
    - B2-a: Why does the author include paragraph ___?
- *The Honest-to-Goodness Truth* by Patricia C. McKissack+
    - A1-a: What lesson does this story teach?
    - A2-a: Using information in the story, write a description of how ___ felt when ___.
    - A2-d: How does ___ change in the story?
    - A3-a: Write a brief summary of this story.
    - A3-b: Summarize the main things that happened in this book.

A4-b: If the author added another paragraph to the end of the story (or article), it would <u>most likely</u> tell about _____. Use information from the story (or article) to support your answer.

■ *The Icky Bug Alphabet Book, The Ocean Alphabet Book, The Boat Alphabet Book*, and many others in this series by Jerry Palotta

A1-c: What is this book/article mainly about?

■ *The Jolly Postman* by Janet and Allan Ahlberg

A3-c: Write a brief summary of this article/informational text

■ *The Keeping Quilt by Patricia Polacco*

C1-a: Think about someone who was [helpful.] Tell how that experience was like the experience of ___ in the story.

D3-a: How does the author/character show that _____ is important to him/her?

■ *The Kid's Book of Questions & Answers: Fascinating Facts about Nature, Science, Space and Much More!* by Ian Graham and Paul Sterry

D2-b: Imagine that you are giving a talk to your class. What two ideas would you include in your speech?

■ *The King Who Rained* and other books in this series by Fred Gwynne

D1-c: How did the author create humor in paragraph ___?

■ *The Kissing Hand* by Audrey Penn

A2-b: What is ___'s main problem in the story? Give details from the story to support your answer.

A2-c: How did ___ solve the problem? Give details from the story to support your answer.

C1-c: Which character in the story would you like to know and why?

■ *The Korean Cinderella* by Shirley Climo+

A2-e: What is the setting of the story? Give details to support your answer.

■ *The Land of Many Colors* by Klamath County YMCA Family Preschool+

A1-b: What is the theme of this story?

C2-a: Which part of the story/article do you think was the most important? Why?

■ *The Librarian of Basra* by Jeanette Winter+

D2-c: Using information from the passage, write an entry that could have appeared in ___'s journal.

D3-a: How does the author/character show that ___ is important to him (or her)?

■ *The Life Cycle of a Butterfly, The Life Cycle of a Flower* and other *Life Cycle* books by Bobbie Kalman

B1-b: What happened at the beginning, middle, and end of the story or informational text?

■ *The Lion Who Wanted to Love* by Giles Andreae and David Wojtowycz

A1-a: What lesson does ___ learn in the story?

A2-d: How does ___ change in the story?

B1-c: Compare these two characters: ___ and ___

■ *The Little Engine that Could* by Watty Piper

A2-b: What is ___'s main problem in the story? Give details from the story to support your answer.

A2-c: How did ___ solve the problem? Give details from the story to support your answer.

- *The Little Island* by Margaret Wise Brown
  - A2-e: What is the setting of the story? Give details to support your answer.
- *The Lotus Seed* by Sherry Garland+
  - A2-e: What is the setting of the story? Give details to support your answer.
  - D2-a: What two questions would you like to ask the author that are not answered in this text?
  - D3-b: How are your customs different from the customs described in this story?
- *The Memory Coat* by Elvira Woodruff+
  - B2-a: Why does the author include paragraph ___?
  - D2-a: What two questions would you like to ask the author that are not answered in this text?
- *The Memory String* by Eve Bunting
  - A2-a: Using information in the story, write a description of how ___ felt when __.
  - A2-d: How does ___ change in the story?
  - A4-b: If the author added another paragraph to the end of the story (or article), it would <u>most likely</u> tell about _____. Use information from the story (or article) to support your answer.
  - C1-c: Which character in the story would you like to know and why?
  - D1-e: Do you think the author made this story believable? Explain.
  - D2-c: Using information from the passage, write an entry that could have appeared in __'s journal.
- *The Name Jar* by Yangsook Choi+
  - A2-d: How does ___ change in the story?
  - A3-a: Write a brief summary of this story.
  - A3-b: Summarize the main things that happened in this book.
  - B1-b: What happened at the beginning, middle, and end of the story or informational text?
  - D3-b: How are your customs different from the customs described in this story?
- *The Other Side* by Jacqueline Woodson+
  - A1-b: What is the theme of this story?
  - A2-b: What is ___'s main problem in the story? Give details from the story to support your answer.
  - A2-c: How did ___ solve the problem? Give details from the story to support your answer.
  - A4-b: If the author added another paragraph to the end of the story (or article), it would <u>most likely</u> tell about _____. Use information from the story (or article) to support your answer.
  - B1-c: Compare these two characters: ___ and ___
  - C2-a: Which part of the story/article do you think was the most important? Why?
  - D2-a: What two questions would you like to ask the author that are not answered in this text?
  - D3-b: How are your customs different from the customs described in this story?

- *The Pain and the Great One* by Judy Blume
    - B1-c: Compare these two characters: ___ and ___
    - B1-d: Can this part of the [story/text] be described as: a definition, a description, an explanation, a conversation, an opinion, an argument, or a comparison? How do you know?
    - C1-a: Think about someone who was [helpful]. Tell how that experience was like the experience of _____ in the story.
- *The Paperbag Princess* By Robert N. Munsch
    - A1-a: What lesson did ___ learn in the story?
    - A2-b: What is ___'s main problem in the story? Give details from the story to support your answer.
    - A2-c: How did ___ solve the problem? Give details from the story to support your answer.
    - A3-a: Write a brief summary of this story.
    - A3-b: Summarize the main things that happened in this book.
    - B1-c: Compare these two characters: ___ and ___
- *The Pig in the Spigot* by Richard Wilbur
    - D1-c: How did the author create humor in paragraph ___?
- *The Polar Express*, *The Wretched Stone* and others by Chris Van Allsburg
    - A4-a: Predict what will happen next in the story.
    - D1-e: Do you think the author made this story believable? Explain.
- *The Princess and the Pizza* by Mary Jane Auch
    - A3-a: Write a brief summary of this story.
    - A3-b: Summarize the main things that happened in this book.
    - D1-e: Do you think the author made this story believable? Explain.
- *The Quiltmaker's Gift* by Jeff Brumbeau
    - A1-a: What lesson does ___ learn in the story?
    - A2-b: What is _____'s main problem in the story? Give details from the story to support your answer.
    - A2-c: How did ___ solve the problem? Give details from the story to support your answer.
- *The Rainbow Fish* by Marcus Pfister
    - A1-a: What lesson does ___ learn in the story?
    - A2-d: How does ___ change in the story?
- *The Relatives Came* by Cynthia Rylant
    - C1-a: Think about someone who was [helpful.] Tell how that experience was like the experience of ___ in the story.
    - D2-c: Using information from the passage, write an entry that could have appeared in __'s journal.
- *The Rough Face Girl* by Rafe Martin
    - B1-a: What caused ___ to happen in the story?
    - B3-a: Prove that character/person is very ___.
- *The Royal Bee* by Frances Park and Ginger Park+
    - A1-b: What is the theme of this story?
    - A2-e: What is the setting of the story? Give details to support your answer.
    - C2-a: Which part of the story/article do you think was the most important? Why?

D2-c: Using information from the passage, write an entry that could have appeared in ___'s journal.

D3-b: How are your customs different from the customs described in this story?

- *The Seashore Book* by Charlotte Zolotow

    D1-a: Choose [2] words from paragraph ___ that help you picture ___.

    D1-b: Choose a simile and explain why the author chose that simile.

- *The Secret Knowledge of Grown-Ups* by David Wisniewski

    A3-c: Write a brief summary of this article/informational text.

- *The Secret Knowledge of Grown-Ups: The Second File* by David Wisniewski

    A3-c: Write a brief summary of this article/informational text.

- *The Story of Jumping Mouse* by John Steptoe

    A2-b: What is ___'s main problem in the story?

    A2-c: How did ___ solve the problem? Give details from the story to support your answer.

    B1-b: What happened at the beginning, middle, and end of the story or informational text?

- *The Story of Ruby Bridges* by Robert Coles+

    B1-c: Compare these two characters: ___ and ___

    B3-a: Prove that character/person is very ___.

    C2-a: Which part of the story/article do you think was the most important? Why?

    C2-d: What was your first reaction to this text? Why?

    D2-a: What two questions would you like to ask the author that are not answered in this text?

- *The Summer My Father was Ten* by Pat Brisson

    A1-a: What lesson does ___ learn in the story?

    C1-a: Think about someone who was [helpful.] Tell how that experience was like the experience of ___ in the story.

    D1-e: Do you think the author made this story believable? Explain.

- *The Three Questions* by Jon J. Muth

    A1-b: What is the theme of this story

    D1-e: Do you think the author made this story believable? Explain.

- *The Tree That Would Not Die* by Ellen Levine

    A1-b: What is the theme of this story?

    D1-d: Give an example of personification in paragraph ___.

- *The Wednesday Surprise* by Eve Bunting

    C1-c: Which character in the story would you like to know and why?

    D2-c: Using information from the passage, write an entry that could have appeared in ___'s journal.

- *The Whales' Song* by Dyan Sheldon+

    D1-a: Choose [2] words from paragraph ___ that help you picture ___.

- *The World Almanac for Kids* published annually by World Almanac

    D2-b: Imagine that you are giving a talk to your class. What two ideas would you include in your speech?

- *The Wretched Stone* by Chris Van Allsburg

    A2-b: What is ___'s main problem in the story? Give details from the story to support your answer.

A2-c: How did ___ solve the problem? Give details from the story to support your answer.

A4-a: Predict what will happen next in the story.

A4-b: If the author added another paragraph to the end of the story (or article), it would <u>most likely</u> tell about _____. Use information from the story or article to support your answer.

D1-e: Do you think the author made this story believable?

■ *The Year I Didn't Go to School* by Giselle Potter+

A2-e: What is the setting of the story? Give details to support your answer.

■ *The Yellow Star* by Carmen Agra Deedy+

A2-b: What is ___'s main problem in the story? Give details from the story to support your answer.

A2-c: How did ___ solve the problem? Give details from the story to support your answer.

C2-a: Which part of the story/article do you think was the most important? Why?

C2-b: Which part of this text was most interesting or surprising to you? Why?

D3-a: How does the author/character show that ___ is important to him (or her)?

■ *This Is the Dream* by Diane Z. Shore and Jessica Alexander+

B1-c: Compare these two characters: ___ and ___.

D2-a: What two questions would you like to ask the author that are not answered in this text?

■ *Thirteen Moons on Turtle's Back* by Joseph Bruchac+

D1-a: Choose [2] words from paragraph ___ that help you picture ___.

■ *Three Paws: The Story of Marley* by Isabela R. Presedo-Floyd

D2-b: Imagine that you are giving a talk to your class. What two ideas would you include in your speech?

■ *Through My Eyes* by Ruby Bridges+

C2-a: Which part of the [story/article] do you think was *most* important? Use information from the [story/article] to explain why you chose that part.

D2-a: What two questions would you like to ask the author that are not answered in this text?

■ *Thunder Cake* by Patricia Polacco

A3-a: Write a brief summary of this story.

A3-b: Summarize the main things that happened in this book.

B1-b: What happened at the beginning, middle, and end of the story or informational text?

C1-b: Make a connection: Show how something that happened in the story is like something that happened in your own life.

C1-c: Which character in the story would you like to know and why?

D2-c: Using information from the passage, write an entry that could have appeared in ___'s journal.

■ *Tomás and the Library Lady* by Pat Mora+

A4-b: If the author added another paragraph to the end of the story (or article), it would <u>most likely</u> tell about _____. Use information from the story (or article) to support your answer.

B2-a: Why does the author include paragraph ___?

C1-c: Which character in the story would you like to know and why?

D2-c: Using information from the passage, write an entry that could have appeared in ___'s journal.

■ *Too Many Tamales* by Gary Soto+

A1-a: What lesson does ___ learn in the story?

A3-a: Write a brief summary of this story.

A3-b: Summarize the main things that happened in this book.

A4-b: If the author added another paragraph to the end of the story (or article), it would <u>most likely</u> tell about _____. Use information from the story (or article) to support your answer.

B1-a: What caused ___ to happen in the story?

C1-c: Which character in the story would you like to know and why?

C2-b: Which part of this text was most interesting or surprising to you? Why?

D1-e: Do you think the author made this story believable? Explain.

D3-b: How are your customs different from the customs described in this story?

■ *Tough Cookie* by David Wisniewski

D1-c: How did the author create humor in paragraph ___?

■ *Town Mouse, Country Mouse* by Jan Brett

D3-b: How are your customs different from the customs described in this story?

■ *Tulip Sees America* by Cynthia Rylant

B1-d: Can this part of the [story/text] be described as: a definition, a description, an explanation, a conversation, an opinion, an argument, or a comparison? How do you know?

■ *Twinnies* by Eve Bunting

C1-b: Make a personal connection: Show how something that happened in the story is like something that happened in your own life.

D1-e: Do you think the author made this story believable? Explain.

■ *Umbrella* by Taro Yashima+

A2-b: What is _____'s main problem in the story? Give details from the story to support your answer.

A2-c: How did ___ solve the problem? Give details to support your answer.

C1-b: Make a personal connection: Show how something that happened in the story is like something that happened in your own life.

■ *Uncle Jed's Barbershop* by Margaree King Mitchell+

A1-b: What is the theme of this story?

■ *Virgie Goes to School with Us Boys* by Elizabeth F. Howard+

A2-b: What is ___'s main problem in the story? Give details from the story to support your answer.

A2-c: How did ___ solve the problem? Give details from the story to support your answer.

D3-a: How does the author/character show that ___ is important to him (or her)?

■ *Water Dance, Cloud Dance, Mountain Dance, and other books by Thomas Locker*

B1-d: Can this part of the [story/text] be described as: a definition, a description, an explanation, a conversation, an opinion, an argument, or a comparison? How do you know?

D1-a: Choose [2] words from paragraph ___ that help you picture ___.

■ *Weather, Volcanoes, Our Solar System* and others by Seymour Simon

    D2-a: What two questions would you like to ask the author that are not answered in this text?

■ *Welcome to the Green House and Welcome to the Sea of Sand by Jane Yolen*

    B1-d: Can this part of the [story/text] be described as: a definition, a description, an explanation, a conversation, an opinion, an argument, or a comparison? How do you know?

    D1-a: Choose [2] words from paragraph ___ that help you picture ___.

■ *Wemberly Worried* by Kevin Henkes

    A2-a: Using information in the story, write a description of how ___ felt when ___.

    B3-a: Prove that character/person is very ___.

    C1-b: Make a connection: Show how something that happened in the story is like something that happened in your own life.

    D1-d: Give an example of personification in paragraph ___.

■ *Weslandia* by Paul Fleischman

    A1-b: What is the theme of this story?

    B1-c: Compare these two characters: ___ and ___

    D1-e: Do you think the author made this story believable? Explain.

■ *What is a Scientist?* by Barbara Lehn

    B1-d: Can this part of the [story/text] be described as: a definition, a description, an explanation, a conversation, an opinion, an argument, or a comparison? How do you know?

    B3-b: Which facts show that ___?

■ *What is Matter?* by Don L. Curry

    B3-b: Which facts show that ___?

■ *What Makes a Magnet?* by Franklyn M. Branley

    B3-b: Which facts show that ___?

■ *What's the Matter with Albert: The Story of Albert Einstein* by Frieda Wishinsky

    B1-c: Compare these two characters: ___ and ___

■ *When I was Little* by Jamie Lee Curtis

    A2-d: How does ___ change in the story?

■ *When I was Young in the Mountains* by Cynthia Rylant

    A2-e: What is the setting of the story? Give details to support your answer.

    C1-d: Using information from the story, explain whether you would want to ___.

    D3-b: How are your customs different from the customs described in this story?

■ *When Marian Sang* by Pam Munoz Ryan+

    A1-a: What lesson does ___ learn in the story?

    A2-a: Using information in the story, write a description of how ___ felt when ___.

    A3-a: Write a brief summary of this story.

    A3-b: Summarize the main things that happened in this book.

    B1-d: Can this part of the [story/text] be described as: a definition, a description, an explanation, a conversation, an opinion, an argument, or a comparison? How do you know?

    C2-a: Which part of the story/article do you think was the most important? Why?

    C2-d: What was your first reaction to this text? Why?

D3-a: How does the author/character show that ___ is important to him (or her)?

■ *When Sophie Gets Angry—Really, Really Angry by Molly Bang*

B1-d: Can this part of the [story/text] be described as: a definition, a description, an explanation, a conversation, an opinion, an argument, or a comparison? How do you know?

C1-b: Make a personal connection: Show how something that happened in the story is like something that happened in your own life.

■ *Where the Wild Things Are by Maurice Sendak*

A4-a: Predict what will happen next in the story.

D1-e: Do you think the author made this story believable? Explain.

■ *Whistle for Willie by Ezra Jack Keats+*

A2-a: Using information in the story, write a description of how ___ felt when ___.

A2-b: What is ___'s main problem in the story? Give details from the story to support your answer.

A2-c: How did ___ solve the problem? Give details from the story to support your answer.

C1-b: Make a personal connection: Show how something that happened in the story is like something that happened in your own life.

■ *White Socks Only by Evelyn Coleman+*

A4-a: Predict what will happen next in the story.

C2-d: What was your first reaction to this text? Why?

D2-a: What two questions would you like to ask the author that are not answered in this text?

D2-c: Using information from the passage, write an entry that could have appeared in ___'s journal.

■ *Whoever You Are by Mem Fox*

A1-b: What is the theme of this story?

■ *Wings by Christopher Myers*

A1-a: What lesson does ___ learn in the story?

B1-c: Compare these two characters: ___ and ___.

■ *With Love, Little Red Hen by Alma Flor Ada*

A3-c: Write a brief summary of this article/informational text.

■ *Young Cornrows Callin Out the Moon by Ruth Forman+*

B1-d: Can this part of the [story/text] be described as: a definition, a description, an explanation, a conversation, an opinion, an argument, or a comparison? How do you know?

C1-d: Using information from the story, explain whether you would want to ___.

■ *Yours Truly, Goldilocks by Alma Flor Ada*

A3-c: Write a brief summary of this article/informational text.

NOTES